# ★ THE RISE OF ★
# AMERICAN
# POPULISM

# ★ THE RISE OF ★
# AMERICAN POPULISM

## A Handbook for
# Radical Patriotism

## Chase Geiser
### Foreword by Alex Jones

Skyhorse Publishing

Skyhorse Publishing ® books may be purchased in bulk at special discounts for sales promotion, corporate gifts, fund-raising, or educational purposes. Special editions can also be created to specifications. For details, contact the Special Sales Department, Skyhorse Publishing, 307 West 36th Street, 11th Floor, New York, NY 10018 or info@skyhorsepublishing.com.

Skyhorse® and Skyhorse Publishing® are registered trademarks of Skyhorse Publishing, Inc.®, a Delaware corporation.

Visit our website at www.skyhorsepublishing.com.
Please follow our publisher Tony Lyons on Instagram @tonylyonsisuncertain.

10 9 8 7 6 5 4 3 2 1

Library of Congress Cataloging-in-Publication Data is available on file.

Jacket design by David Ter Avanesyan

Print ISBN: 978-1-5107-8136-8
Ebook ISBN: 978-1-5107-8137-5

Printed in the United States of America

**To InfoWars**
While other networks lie to you about what's happening now,
InfoWars tells you the truth about what's happening next.

# CONTENTS

# FOREWORD

---

## BY ALEX JONES

We're living in an era where the very foundations of our great nation are under threat. The globalist agenda, driven by the elite and their puppet mainstream media, is working tirelessly to erode our freedoms, silence our voices, and rewrite the narrative of our history. But we, the people, have a weapon against this tyranny: the truth.

This book is that weapon.

Chase Geiser dives deep into the heart of American Populism, dissecting its roots, its rise, and its critical role in our nation's future. He unveils the uncomfortable truths that the power-hungry elite don't want you to know. *The Rise of American Populism* exposes the corrupt system that's rigged against the common man, the silent majority who have been sidelined and suppressed for far too long.

It's time to wake up, America! The globalists fear an informed and united populace, and that's exactly what we need to become. This book lays bare the strategies and manipulations used by those in power to control us, to turn us against each other, and to keep us in the dark.

But there's hope. We can win the InfoWar and the truth unleashed from these pages will go down in history as a crucial part of our victory. Chase Geiser doesn't just highlight the problem for readers. He offers solutions. It's a clarion call for action, urging us to reclaim our rights, our voice, and our country. It's a road map for restoring the true spirit of America, an America where freedom, individuality, and the pursuit of happiness aren't just ideas, but realities.

In these pages, you'll find the truth that's been hidden from you. You'll discover how to fight back against the globalist agenda and how to join the growing movement of populist patriots who are taking a stand for their country.

This isn't just another book. It's a call to action for every person with America in their heart. As patriots, there is no call we leave unanswered. Let this book ignite the fire of American Populism within you. Not only will you find that you gain critical information from this book, but you'll be inspired to do what needs to be done to save this country.

Let's stand together as true patriots, armed with the truth and united in our cause. The future of our nation depends on it. The battle for America's soul is on, and it's a battle we must win if we are to achieve total victory in the InfoWar.

# ★ THE RISE OF ★
# AMERICAN
# POPULISM

CHAPTER 1

# AN AMERICAN VILLAIN

———

On the night of the election in 2016, Americans celebrated the future of the nation excitedly. Against all odds, the Political Right had taken total control of the government and seemed unstoppable.

By the time Biden was inaugurated in 2021, American voices were being silenced by censorship, America's treasury had become an indebted abyss, and Americans were faced with astounding levels of personal debt, unemployment, lockdowns, vaccine mandates, mask mandates, and countless other betrayals of their rights by the very people sworn to protect them.

All that America had created had been sold out to enemies both foreign and domestic. American wealth was exported in stimulus packages and COVID-19 relief bills. It was exploited and used by the Political Left to buy favor among a helpless and vulnerable base. The crippling inflationary measures, taxation, and subjugation of Americans by violating the rights promised us by our sacred Constitution have rendered it seemingly impossible for America to ever be reborn. So what's in store for America now? Will there be a second coming for America?

There will be the selling out of our property, the enslavement of our working class by impoverishing it to the point of total government dependence. The actions of the Political Left have not served the American people but instead have contributed to their very desperation.

We've allowed our military to be consumed by critical theory and "wokeism", and we've weakened to cater to the emotional sensitivity of those who don't even love their own country enough to truly fight for it.

We've lost the sovereignty of our nation, and our leaders continue to exploit our past glory by exchanging the fruits of our accomplishments for favor among globalist special interests. We've lost our financial independence by leaving the gold standard, then recklessly exacerbating the inflation of the dollar to the brink of collapse. We're left with the likes of the World Economic Forum, NATO, the United Nations, and the January 6 Committee, so that we no longer have a politically independent United States of America.

We allowed ourselves to be morally humiliated. We destroyed our own culture and betrayed everything we previously understood to be immutably true. In the face of this rapid decline, the leftists claim that their policies have resulted in great gains for American lives. What gains?! Working Americans aren't finding any positive change in their practical lives—only increased gas prices, unaffordable houses, crippling debt, and no reason to think that things will be better anytime soon.

Some may say, "Well unemployment has reached record lows." I'm compelled to ask the question, "Was the total collapse of our culture, our dollar, our economy, and our dignity necessary for that?"

Others on the Left say that leftist policies have resulted in the protection of American rights, that the people are finally being represented and overcoming a fascist right. Yet, we see that the leftists have been growing in power all this time, and no leftist leaders have seemingly asked the opinion of the American people once. Instead, they falsify polls and lie about American sentiments to deceive the American people into believing the Left has the moral high ground.

We commit ourselves to globalist organizations and deals wherein we pay much more than our fair share without complaint to our foreign "allies" who exploit our great resources and contribute nothing in return. Who agreed to these deals? Who supported the World Economic Forum? Who signed off on giving foreign aid to our enemies? The people? No! Instead, it was the leftist political machine that one day proclaimed itself our government.

Sure, the people elected the Senators and the Representatives, but only from options presented and approved by the establishment political class. If you don't think the establishment chooses the candidates, just look what the Republican Party did to the great patriot Robby Starbuck in Tennessee. Furthermore, we did not elect the intelligence officer reading your emails or texts. We did not elect the hundreds of thousands busily at work for the ATF, FBI, CIA, IRS, NSA, or DOJ working against the best interests of Americans and consequently against the best interests of America itself.

After the inauguration of the Biden Regime, the Left proclaimed that finally we had been freed of tyranny, we had finally overthrown the insurrectionist and stopped an attempted coup, we finally had true freedom! Another invisible reality the Left swears to have manifested. It's true that Americans can walk down the street, we can go to work or wherever we'd like to go, or go to a meeting of like-minded friends. Sure, Americans have their freedoms. But generally, if we know what's good for us, we will keep our mouths shut when it comes to voicing our concerns. Now, Americans must be incredibly careful not to say anything that might insult the leftist regime or its members, lest they face losing their social media presence, their careers, and even their freedom.

If you're asking yourself, "Who is responsible for the rapid decline of America?" then simply ask yourself, "Who is benefiting from the weakening of America?" It's the banks, the *leftist* billionaires, the elites, the corrupt politicians, and their class of minions who make the policies that ensure the value of their investments will grow beyond the capabilities of any ordinary American's investments.

The Left calls this corruption the result of capitalism, but American capitalism has been as good as dead for over a century now. What the Left calls capitalism isn't capitalism at all. They criticize fascism and call it capitalism to sabotage and poison our culture into shame, humiliation, and self-hatred. They do this in an effort to make Americans believe that the ownership of private property, personal success, and the belief in individual rights are fascist.

It is not capitalism to remove the dollar from the gold standard and print money indiscriminately until the middle class is taxed out of existence. That's leftism. It is not capitalism when capital is only available to major corporations who align themselves with the principles of globalist organizations like the World Economic Forum, NATO, or the UN. That's fascism. It is not capitalism when globalists have acquired or priced out small businesses, outsourced all manufacturing, taxed the middle class to the point of living paycheck to paycheck, and paid our foreign enemies with those taxes in the form of "foreign aid." That's leftist fascism. Frankly, it's *treason*.

The leftist political elite isn't getting poorer. Leftists are physically inflating more quickly than our dollar and forcing us to call them beautiful despite our most basic human instinct to be disgusted. If you go to any job site in America you won't find a leftist working in the sun by the sweat of their brow; you'll find them sitting aimlessly in their offices at university or quietly munching their favorite pastry in their HR department cubicle, or in their overpriced San Francisco apartment excitedly reviewing a patriot's social media content for terms of service violations.

These leftists are the political class and they have done nothing to help the most vulnerable in America. Instead they have exploited the problems of struggling Americans by promising to solve them in exchange for political support. When their supporters ask them, "Why is nothing improving?" the leftists either say, "Things are better and you're just too blind to see" or, "Your fellow Americans and neighbors are betraying you and making political change difficult or impossible for us."

They have suffered nothing for America, but America has suffered much for them. Too much.

The American people are beginning to wake up, and opposition to the enemies of America is growing. Americans are realizing the facts. They're beginning to pursue the system that poisons them. *True Americans will one day soon inspire into action hundreds of millions of Americans along with them.* The leftist political class is beginning to see that their enemies are growing in numbers—and when the American people recognize the momentum of our America First Movement, it will be the end for the globalist political class.

When this populist American idea is grasped by a movement which can unite it with a regained patriotic resistance, then the system that has abused our people will fall apart. The Left's past lies force them to constantly resort to new lies, and their new lies are leading them to no salvation.

## But Can the Right Save America?

What has the Political Right accomplished for its people? The Republican Party means well, but it hasn't saved America from her enemies because it has failed to understand what's really going on. Frankly, the Right still fails to see the true danger today even after what we've seen from the Left since Election Day in 2016.

These leaders continue to believe that restoring America to her former glory is simply a matter of being elected to the Senate or to the House of Representatives, or of being appointed to positions in the various three-letter agencies or in the judiciary. They believe that a leftist political victory means nothing more than some modest or correctable damage to the economic welfare of working Americans. They have yet to realize that a leftist political victory in the United States means that American lives will be lost, persecuted, tortured, impoverished, imprisoned, chastised, banished, raped, trafficked, indoctrinated, enslaved, and subjugated.

The Political Right *still* doesn't understand that the leftists won't stop at destroying their enemies. They'll destroy every semblance of what was once considered American. The manifestation of leftist ideals always ends with "Join or Die."

As a result of their naive attitude toward the Political Left, the Political Right's actions are only ever small, restrained, reluctant and half-hearted. The Political Right may love America and wish to save her, but they can never decide on any great attack or action because they haven't yet determined whether there is a great threat.

The Right has yet to overcome its discomfort with a true American Populist Movement because they are too concerned with being perceived as authoritarian, dictatorial, or despotic. They are unwilling to acknowledge the great truth that American populism is inherently antithetical to the concept of tyranny, because nothing truly American can ever be tyrannical.

As for those who say, "There are countless examples of American tyranny," they are confusing America with the United States.

They should find the courage to call upon everyone among us who has an American heart in the fight against the common enemy of all true Americans, the globalist Left.

But even with the most intense courage and will of the Political Right, it won't prevail unless the America it seeks to build truly corresponds to the welfare of the American people.

That the enlightenment of the Founding Fathers was able to manifest in the Constitution of the United States of America depended solely on the fact that, though these powerful men could undoubtedly have decided any random outcome for the American people they did not do so, but made their decisions influenced and supported by one thought alone, concern for the welfare of the American people. It was this that led to the establishment of a great nation and a government by the *consent* of the governed.

The Political Right has completely forgotten that leftism even democracy itself, is fundamentally not American. The Republicans themselves have forgotten the meaning of *republic*—the very form of government a Republican, by definition, is meant to support.

The leftist democracy has always been only a means to destroy true American values. The Right doesn't consider the fact that in a democracy the majority can legally violate the rights of any minority and consequently any individual. The leftist understands this and knows that those who control public opinion control the people themselves, and that controlling public opinion can be done by anyone who can master the art of lying.

Finally, the Political Right has failed to understand that it is not enough to know the truth; there must also be a will to act on it and a courage to speak it—something neither the Political Right nor the Political Left seem to be capable of to this day.

So, there can be only two outcomes for America. The people will not go on forever supporting political leaders who compromise or seek moderate approaches to radical problems. Soon, Americans will turn to those who have most consistently predicted the coming tragedy and who have visibly fought against it. That party is either going to be perceived as the Political Left, which will lead America to her final death—globalism—or it will be the Political Right; when the people have reached a state of total despair, when they have lost all faith, when they become determined to fight uncompromisingly for America, this will mark the beginning of a resistance by which America's second coming may be possible. There will be either total American victory, or total American destruction by globalist hands.

The realization of this truth resulted in the formation of the America First movement and ultimately inspired me and millions of others to desperately seek a way to save our country and our people. If the America First movement seeks to gain power and save this nation it must have a total understanding of the following truths.

First, populism and patriotism are inseparable. Only leftists claim otherwise because they themselves know it to be true. In an effort to weaken their opposition, the Political Left has exercised the use of Marxism and critical theory to demonize what in reality are virtues. They have said that populism is hate and that patriotism itself is a principle only the patriarchy, racists, sexists, bigots, and insurrectionists support.

The America First movement isn't really a movement in and of itself. It's a value, a principle, that is part of an even greater movement: populist patriotism. To be a populist means to harbor an overwhelming love of country and countrymen to the point of a willingness to live for it. To be a patriot means to act and live in a way that never betrays that love.

Therefore every true American is your equal regardless of wealth, race, religion, or other immutable quality, and in order to truly love America and the American people it is not enough to stand by quietly and bask in our affection. Love is manifest only by action! By work! And just as you prove faithful to your country by the work you do to contribute to your community, so you are loved by the work your fellow patriot does for you. Another's great success is the greatest honor they can bestow upon their country and not something to envy but something to be grateful for.

Leftist values fundamentally differ from American values. The true American regards work as an American duty to their country, while the leftist regards work as a means of exploitation. The leftist never works as a productive member of society for any reason but to dominate others. The leftist uses and enjoys other people's work, and so leftism itself is an inherent cause of American entropy.

That being said, populist patriotism does not advocate self-sacrifice or collectivism but instead it is the opposite. Your love of your country is worthless if you have sacrificed your integrity, for then it isn't true love from a complete person but empty love from a shell of a man. In fact, it is your duty to pursue economic prosperity, and therefore it is necessary that there be maximum political freedom in America to enable working Americans to reach self-actualization—for you cannot become the best version of yourself if you don't have the freedom to do what it takes. The Political Left would rather have everyone be equally poor than unequally prosperous. They don't want to liberate Americans from the bonds of oppression but to subjugate them like cattle. They oppose freedom because freedom empowers the individual and empowered individuals cannot be subjugated. We therefore must recognize that freedom can only be a consequence of power and that the source of power is the will, and that the will of populist patriots is the people's power over the state, not the state's power over the people.

The will of the people must be radical. Even the smallest minority can achieve astounding results if it is inspired by a zealous will to act. *History is made by radical minorities—the greatest minority of all being the individual.* Just knowing the truth is not enough. In fact, knowing is meaningless if it is not met with action.

This is the spirit of populist patriotism. It is a movement inevitably conceived because of these truths and because Americans are facing the oppressive nightmare of the Left.

When we demanded the truth, the Left called us liars. When we demanded justice, they called us criminals. When we demanded liberty, they called us oppressors. And when we called ourselves patriots, they called us insurrectionists.

I would like to ask those who called us liars, criminals, oppressors, and insurrectionists, "What can you give the American people to believe in?"

*Nothing at all, because you don't even believe in America itself.*

The most powerful thing we can give the American people is the hope that the will of patriots is fated to save America. If all who love their country do their duty for it, then America's second coming is inevitable.

## CHAPTER 2

# AN AMERICAN HERO

The war against America began almost a hundred years ago with the advent of leftist thought in response to the Great Depression. The New Deal, in all its evil splendor, enslaved the individual to the elite in the guise of the greater good. The Left's approach to the global economic crisis, a crisis which they catalyzed themselves, was to seize property from Americans, including all privately owned gold, and justify the enforcement with what was branded as the moral imperative of altruism. This enforced altruism is truly nothing more than theft: theft from those for whom it purports to benefit, theft from Americans for the sake of globalist war and the pocketbooks of the political class—a class which branded itself as American leadership, which has clearly and definitely become a class apart from America itself and deeply foreign to the interests of every true American.

It didn't happen due to one specific instance of bad policy or evil intention, but increasingly over time as a result of desperation among a people who have been intentionally confused, exploited, demonized, impoverished, and robbed. Little by little the political class created a conglomeration of power, power that had been taken from the American people themselves—for power can neither be created or destroyed, it merely changes form.

The vast process of exploitation continued with the departure of the United States from the gold standard, rendering the world's reserve currency a true fiat, left to massive money printing at the discretion of private centralized bankers at the Federal Reserve. Printing allowed the political class to steal from the American class without notice as the dollars were not taken from their accounts but instead rendered less valuable as other dollars were made and given to members of the political class via the military industrial complex, social programs, foreign aid, and every mechanism imaginable that could get money from the federal government without having to earn it in the American market. A political industrial complex that encompassed and transcended the military industrial complex was formed.

Thus a massive population of political parasites was bred, and these "Americans" were not stopped by true Americans whose duty it was to preserve the integrity of the West. Through this exploitation, the entire American economy and the Stock Exchange became dependent on the printing of money, which is the robbery of the American people, to sustain itself indefinitely toward an inevitable collapse.

The leaders of these organizations, contractors, "nonprofits," NGOs, and committees were undoubtedly leftists, and if they were not at first leftists they gradually became leftists, for one cannot commit evil long without becoming fundamentally evil himself. Even those who appeared to have America's interests in mind, even those who considered themselves true American patriots, only served to win the trust of the American people so they could stab them in the back immediately following the words, "Nothing to see here."

Then America began the gradual split into a polarized two-party system and philosophy: the Political Right and the Political Left, which are to be distinguished from the American Right and the American Left. The Political Right, in an effort to consolidate support among the American Right, vocally supported and fought for the preservation of

American values, her Constitution, individualism, and liberty, despite the gradual erosion of their positions by the enactment of Marxist policy over the course of decades.

The Political Left, in an attempt to consolidate the support of the American Left, proceeded to vocally support the vulnerable and working-class Americans who, in their struggle and desperation, looked to them to keep them housed, educated, employed, and cared for despite the fact that the Marxist Political Left had no intention of easing their pain, for their suffering was the very foundation of leftist power in America.

And so, through the leftists' exploitation of the American vulnerable, they won their hearts and minds by seeming to be their champion to their face while perpetuating their existence and increasing their struggle behind their back. So, in the minds of the American Left the need for the Political Left was ever growing. Thus, the more Americans who struggled, the more power the American Left acquired; and the more power the Political Left acquired, the more concession the Political Right gave, finally manifesting the single party state we see today—deceiving the American people on all facets of the political spectrum.

The same process took place in Europe and other places of the world before its infectious and malignant roots took hold in America—and we've seen the cultural and political ruin of every nation that it has touched. Hundreds of years ago when a people were abused by such great political corruption, they would simply pack up their lives and place themselves farther west; but today there is no farther west to go, and America remains the last stand and the last hope for freedom in the world, as true Americans are the only people in history to be inherently and fundamentally aware of the self-evident truths of their right to life, liberty, and the pursuit of happiness. But these Americans have to act now, for it may be too late by the end of this very decade.

The Left has sabotaged the American identity by consistently fight-ing for democracy, for democratic values, and their perpetual use of these terms and this advocacy has been so subtle and yet saturated that even the Political Right champion democracy and democratic values, despite the fact that *democracy isn't once mentioned in our Constitution and America has never been and was never intended to be a democracy.* We are a republic, a republic that represents the interests of the people while simultaneously checking the power of the mob to overrule the rights of the individual American and thereby subjugate all Americans. By touting democracy, the leftists have succeeded in subjugating America while the American people remained unaware of who they were a subject to or that they were even subjugated at all.

Ultimately, this subjugation, this "democracy" only serves the inter-ests of the political class—a class that will never serve the interests of Americans and inevitably must yield to globalism for Marxism, which does not recognize the sovereignty of the individual, cannot recognize the sovereignty of a nation (for a nation of subjects becomes the subject of nations, and no Marxist nation has sustained itself without expand-ing like a Ponzi scheme). The Soviet Union collapsed due to the stag-nation of its expansion and exploitation of new peoples. China nearly collapsed during the Great Leap Forward and ultimately resorted to deceiving and taking advantage of America by taking her aid and her manufacturing and making her people dependent upon it for virtu-ally every object sold in the United States. North Korea hangs on by a thread and leans on China like a drunk brother while China recently took hold of Hong Kong and has its eyes on Taiwan next to perpetuate its status as a global power.

The political class has disguised its true loyalty to globalism by per-petuating the illusion of a two-party state in America. This has given the American people the impression that while one party is in power, the other is fighting to take power back and overcome that party. When they win in the midterms or the presidential elections, the cycle repeats and the party formerly in power now appears to fight for its base. In reality neither party fights for any true American base, but only to perpetuate the power monopoly of the political class.

In the face of this we see one party that outwardly advocates for freedom or liberty while the other advocates for democracy and equality, which has now been psychologically merged into the notion of equity. The Political Right cries out in support of liberty while legalizing the governmental espionage of the American people, the redistribution of their wealth across the world, and the continued devaluing of our money—all while their base feels their political leaders are their only hope.

Meanwhile, the Political Left cries out in support of democracy to its base, claiming to advocate for the liberation of America's vulnerable and disenfranchised. They claim to support the minority communities who were liberated from the bonds of slavery and to fight for those who have been victims of prejudice, hatred, exploitation, and bigotry—all while enacting policies that further enslave and subjugate their base by rendering their dollars worthless and furthering their dependence on the state.

Through this, both elements of the political industrial complex have deceived and exploited the American class, humiliated them by shaming any love of country or culture as bigotry, and destroyed their families by inflating the currency such that both parents have to work. As a result of this, families were forced to hand their children to the state at younger and younger ages, which ultimately resulted in generations of Americans raised by the state and indoctrinated to willful subjugation of themselves, and their adamant subjugation of any American who has peered for a moment into his own soul and found the great truth that every American will find upon looking within: that every American is a sovereign nation in and of himself. And no one has a right to his life, his identity, his work, or anything that he manifests through the miracle that is the imagination of a vision for himself and who has the audacity to manifest it.

This principle has been the fundamental reason for America's inherent resistance to leftism, for the principle is the foundation of our great Constitution—a document that has singlehandedly made the explicit hostile Marxist takeover of America politically impossible. It could not be done through revolution because, thanks to capitalism and the protection of private property, her people were not impoverished enough to incentivize rising up in arms. It could not be done immediately through radical policies because most explicitly Marxist policies were constitutionally illegal. And so, it has been done culturally, through the corporate media of the state, the slow erosion of the strength of our Constitution, the devaluation of our dollar, and the total compromise of all culture and entertainment, from the music we hear, the movies we watch, the games we play, and the behavior and ideals that we idolize.

The Political Right's expansion and empowerment of the federal government in conjunction with The Political Left's crippling of the American people has been a great success in their effort to take everything from us in the blink of an eye.

But the leftists have one great adversary yet to be overcome: the populist patriot, the American individual. The concepts of the American individual, the American populist, and the American patriot are the holy trinity of Americanism. They are symbiotic and one cannot live without the other. As long as there is one American with America in his heart, there is hope that America will manifest in the world again. This poses a great threat to the leftist resolve, which is why they have taken every step to make it impossible for true Americans to come together in the love of their country and themselves to reclaim America.

They have censored Americans on social media, lied to them in the media, humiliated them and degraded them. Called them morally inferior, intellectually incapable, weak, and ultimately so alone as to have no hope. They have isolated us in the name of public health, arrested us and decried us as traitors, silenced us, impoverished us, disarmed us, and divided us.

The leftists can divide America, and they can isolate true Americans from one another, but they can never isolate an individual from himself, for this cannot be done by force but must be done with consent. And if true Americans reclaim their own identities and live according to American values, they will be drawn together as a blazing star bends light toward itself, as if to say, "We are the masters of our fate. We are the captains of our souls."

The leftist will always champion the sacrifice of the individual to the state and ultimately the sacrifice of the state to the world. For if Americans sacrifice themselves to the mob they can never truly come together as one living being but only in one massive grave. Even if there remains air in their lungs there is no life in the souls of those who sacrifice themselves willfully to the will of other men, to the political class, to globalism.

From Benjamin Franklin to Steve Bannon, true Americans have all united in their recognition that the leftist is not only fundamentally un-American—and therefore inherently an enemy of all American people—but is America's greatest enemy as long as he is empowered by us.

The leftist exploited the opportunity to subjugate America by implanting itself in our schools and entertainment and ultimately converting the masses to Marxist thought. Once the educational system was infected with its plague, the disease began to take hold in our corporations and seeped into the private sector of our nation. And so we must ask ourselves: what is their final goal?

In order for Marxism to take a final hold over America, it must bring the people to a place of total desperation. A culmination of manufactured crises such as the pandemic will continue to unfold. The next targets will be our currency, which as it stands has been greatly weakened but has yet to collapse. The leftists mean for it to collapse, because once Americans have nothing they will give everything, even themselves, over to the state in the desperate hope that the state will have the power and intention to aid its people.

This process to weaken America to the point of total subjugation, which has not been seen since the first American escaped the shackles of despotism and set foot on our shores, will end suddenly when one American among us rises to the duty to lead our people from bondage and inspires other true Americans to resist the globalists who call themselves our countrymen.

This threat is constantly in the mind of the leftist. It is why they have done all they can to deplatform and assassinate the voices of all opposition. They will endeavor to make any populist patriotism look like the foolishness of the uneducated, or the greed of a fascist, or the bigotry of the patriarchy. The leftist must destroy America within the hearts and minds of all Americans, because the leftist can't create anything of his own. He can only take from others who have created. Marxism has never founded a nation, only revolutionized it. It has never sustained itself, only perpetuated itself through expansion, and once expansion became impossible, it collapsed. The leftist has nothing to give to America—only the power to take from America. It was American patriots only who created this country, and it is American patriots only who can reclaim it.

One has to be neither a Donald Trump supporter nor a critic to admit the obvious fact that if he accomplished one thing it was the exposure of the corruption within the state and the extent to which Marxism ideals and tactics have truly taken hold in the United States. It became clear during the campaign of 2016 that the political elite could commit crimes and get away with them, when no justice was brought to the Clinton regime for its corruption or to the DNC for its illegal and ironically antidemocratic actions against Bernie Sanders in the Democratic primary.

It was made even clearer when America was shaken to find that Trump had won the election. The corporate media had convinced Americans that a Clinton victory would be resounding, and the moment that Trump was announced the president-elect there was no other tenable explanation as to why the polls had been so wrong—other than that the polls were not polls at all but *lies* all along.

Then, the Left proceeded to falsify documents and implement the Patriot Act's powers—powers created by the Political Right—to not only spy on the Trump administration but to accuse him of Russian collusion in an effort to unseat him, an act of treason that has been proven to have taken place.

We continued to see an onslaught of similar attacks over the course of years not only on the presidency but on Americans themselves who were accused of being white supremacists, terrorists, Nazis, bigots, privileged, sexist, and every terrible character a person could be. When the pandemic came to our shores from a foreign adversary, it was found that not only had the political class funded and profited from many of the entities responsible for the creation and spread of the disease, but they continued to profit from the response to it, which was overwhelmingly disproportionate to the threat itself and culminated in a greater injustice than the pandemic itself. Not only did millions of businesses close, but states acted in such a way as to change voting procedures and lie to such an extent that regardless of whether the 2020 election was legitimate or not, there was no way that either outcome would have been trusted wholeheartedly by any American. Further, the Political Right failed to prevent this great tragedy of trust and failed to protect those Americans who were silenced, fired, or imprisoned for expressing their sentiments throughout the coming months and on January 6.

Yet, the exposure of the leftist infestation of our sacred country is not enough in and of itself to awaken America's second coming. Two things must unfold before an awakening is complete: first, increased economic distress, and second, increased political division within.

They endeavor to divide Americans among themselves by having the American Right blame the American Left and the American Left blame the American Right for the increasing desperation among our people, when in reality the true culprit is the political class manifest in the false two-party system of the Political Right and Political Left.

How do they do this? Through the corporate press, which is no longer an independent corporate press but a private political press, and which maintains its private autonomy by catering to the political class to earn and maintain their affection. This is not only corrupt but is the definition of fascism, as the political class has succeeded in seizing the means of information.

While America is subjected to constant lying and dominance by disinformation, they are led completely astray. Those who believe the lies are lost because nothing they believe is true, while those who know they are being lied to know not where to look for truth. Slowly, those who do not believe the lies are beginning to identify the true culprits of deceit as the political class working at the behest of leftists who are selling out America to their globalist peers. If this gradual awakening continues to take place, over time it will gain speed and shine a light so bright on the masses that no remaining Americans will be capable of closing their eyes—and the closer Americans come to the Second Enlightenment, the more extreme the means of leftism will become to subvert it.

Even today, if one criticizes the political press or its narrative, they are demonized. If one criticizes critical theory and its rotting of our culture, they are a bigot. If an American claims they are being censored, they are silenced. If they claim to love our country, they are a patriarch.

If they achieve success they are an elitist or if they resist the hijacking of their children they are considered unfit to raise children. Imagine if Americans hadn't been resisting leftism all these years? We would already be lost beyond repair! Unfortunately, the American people are much too complicit, for if we had resisted the squandering of our country and our culture long ago we never would have arrived at the crisis before us.

The day is coming—and there will be an American reckoning—because the manifestation of all leftist ideology is "Join or Die," and every true American carries within his heart the sacred ultimatum, "Give me liberty or give me death."

Our leaders know that unrest is accumulating in this country, and despite every effort they make to trample all resistance, by expanding the power and scope of the government, they accomplish nothing but the devaluation of our currency to the point of worthlessness, where not even $1 million will be enough to pay a working class American a day's wage. Soon the day is coming when this must stop, and America must be prepared for that day when it comes.

Now, America is approaching a political environment virtually identical to those seen in North Korea, Russia, Cuba, and all Marxist civilizations. The grip placed on the neck of America will only tighten as more Americans wake up to the only rational and moral ideal: populist patriotism.

Whether our great movement is called Populist Patriotism, America First, or by any other name, it's a fact that everywhere you look in America, the reawakening of the nation is happening, and America's second coming will be the most unified movement in the history of our great country. In every small town of America you can hear the murmurings of this movement begin to take form, and soon the truth will manifest in a call so clear, so loud, it will be as if the very angels of God themselves have returned to announce a complete and perfect justice once and for all. Americans know that America can stand as a nation only if Americans can stand against the globalist political class. Each American's most dangerous enemy is the globalist, for nothing is more antithetical to individualism than globalism.

Every truly American concept leads to populism, for populism is the love of a nation's people, and one cannot honestly claim to love the people and advocate for the state at their expense.

Americans have always and will always know no greater thing than the prosperity of their people, the exceptionalism of this great experiment founded on the blood of patriots who had everything in life to lose but clung to the hope that that which is worth living for is worth dying for as well. We have prided ourselves for three hundred years in our advocacy for the individual, for the protection of the individual's rights and property, for the celebration of their success and not the shaming of it. Even when our nation was plagued with the great sin of slavery, our Constitution guided our nation away from this crime toward the only true American outcome—emancipation. Even when our nation struggled with the sin of racism and unequal protection for racial minorities under the law, our American integrity corrected this transgression and repented from this evil.

As a result, the nation with the greatest peace among religions is the nation with the greatest freedom of religion. The nation with the greatest peace among dissenting neighbors was the same that had the greatest protection of speech. Where there is freedom, there is peace, and where there is peace, there is prosperity, and nothing in the world is more important to true Americans than freedom and the infinite potential it gives every individual to become the best version of themselves. This is populist patriotism! For the love of the individual is the love of country, and no greater America can exist than one composed of Americans achieving greatness.

This America can only exist when it is not divided into the political class versus the working class, but when every American is given the freedom to do what it takes to become the best version of themselves—to reach their capacity and discover how great that capacity truly is.

It is the very idea of America that the leftists are most afraid of, and that is why they are desperately doing everything possible to quarantine the people from who it is their destiny to become. Of all people in America who dream, it is our youth who dream the most, for they have only the future before them. The leftists know the youth have the greatest potential to save America, and that is why they seek to corrupt them as soon as they take their first steps. The leftist knows that a child who steps into his own cannot be led to the slaughter.

The leftist knows that the long established political parties can be swayed by the promise of power or riches, and these party leaders are so blinded by their infinite narcissism that the very concept of populism is alien to them. The people will be the ones who must finally awaken them. Just look at both parties and their leaders with their silk hair and smug smiles happily preaching on controlled media the lies they believe Americans to be stupid enough to believe. These party leaders are no threat to any of America's enemies, let alone the leftist operatives within, because our leaders don't recognize how advanced the leftist corruption of America is. As a result, they have become the political class themselves. They have become leftists even as they believe they are of the Right. They have become globalists even as they believe they are patriots. Why? Because those who compromise become compromised.

To those who say, "We need to reach across the aisle" or "We need bipartisan support" or "We need more moderates back in leadership," I say 1,776 times, "No!" What other purpose of this advocacy for moderation that we see from our leaders can there be but to weaken every

American and therefore weaken America itself so as to neutralize the last threat to the globalist political class: Americans themselves.

Internationally, we are a humiliated country with a babbling gerontocracy, an economy that is a shadow of its former glory, and a military committed to inclusiveness more than victory. We are no longer seen as a threat, and our enemies are emboldened. Only one thing remains for the globalist political class to achieve global conquest: the assassination of the American spirit, and ultimately the imprisonment, financial ruin, or execution of every American with the audacity to live as a true American. We know this because not long ago the war on terrorism was a war in distant lands, yet now domestic terrorism is deemed the greatest threat to national security—but I see only Americans among us.

Not only are pro-American organizations and their members placed on watchlists by the unchecked fourth branch of government that is the intelligence community but the very same entities that claim that our populist patriots are committing acts of domestic terrorism are the ones who infiltrate and corrupt these honest organizations in order to incite them to violence—namely, the false-flag kidnapping plot of a governor and the "insurrection" on January 6, which was coaxed by undercover operatives of the political class and welcomed with open doors (literally).

Just as the political class has sponsored and executed countless regime changes around the world, as well as civil wars, assassinations, and human rights violations, so they turn their tactics and experience on the American people and incite the American Right and the American Left to riot against both the state and each other, leaving ordinary citizens too afraid to voice their concern or even leave their homes because they believe that if they keep their head down their lives, their homes, and their jobs will be safe. They believe if they stand up to the leftists' stoking violence in our own communities they will be deplatformed, canceled, and shunned, but the alternative outcome is far more terrifying. The consequences of complacency are far greater than the consequences of looking the enemy in the eyes and saying, "No more." For if the leftists take the sacred stronghold of America, then the world is lost until the total manifestation of globalism results in its inevitable outcome: total collapse.

We know that the disinformation governance board that was announced the very day of this writing is nothing less than a means to silence all opposition. We know too that no effort to silence every American, even the very last American heroes, will be spared; there will be no accountability for those sworn to hold the enemies of America accountable, for these entities have been compromised themselves. That's why we as populist patriots, true Americans, make the imperative distinction between America and the United States—between America and the government. When some politician grandstands against us and calls us traitors or insurrectionists, we are, as you should be, unshaken. Our loyalty to America is self-evident in the lives we have lived, the wars many of us have fought in for our country, the jobs we have worked, the taxes we have paid, the Americans we have raised, and the injustices we have, up unto this point, misguidedly tolerated for the sake of maintaining the peace.

Populist patriots are convinced that when this American conflict reaches a climax, Americans—out of love of their country and bitterness for the injustices committed upon her people—will rise up and recognize the enemy among us and say, "Never again." Then a true American renaissance will rise from the ashes of injustice and establish a greater freedom than has ever existed on this land, a greater prosperity than the earth has ever witnessed, and an unlimited potential to manifest our very fate itself. Many Americans, in the search for the true culprit of our desperation, mistakenly believe that it is their neighbor on the Left who votes for the Democrats or our neighbor on the Right who votes for the Republicans, but I implore you not to alienate your fellow Americans in one word and decry the political class in the same breath. Instead, graciously tolerate the errors of your neighbor, for they know not what they do. If we tolerate the honest mistakes of the American class we will have the whole of America on our side when the real enemy presents itself at our door.

We, populist patriots, who have for years decried the managed destruction of America, have been abused, insulted, slandered, imprisoned, deplatformed, and fired, can never give up, for it will be all in vain if we surrender all that is worth fighting for. Just as our forefathers set sail in one direction, due west, to find America, so now there is one path forward to rediscover her again. We know that there will be much adversity to overcome, and that this war will not be fought in the courts, or in the Senate or in the House of Representatives, or in the West Wing, but in the heart of every American with the will not only to die for his country, but to live for it.

The political class trains their youth to be politically correct, to use delicate words and speak eloquently for hours on end without saying anything at all, but the only way to raise a true American is to be strong in the face of adversity, not overwhelmingly sensitive to it! For when the real adversity falls upon all America, and it inevitably will, there will be no safe space for the vulnerable among us who could otherwise have developed the strength of character to withstand the onslaught and face the enemy with integrity by acting as an American hero would act, and not just to rely on stronger men to rise to the occasion.

If we begin to think freely we discover the truth within ourselves. If we summon the smallest courage to look carefully we can see a glimpse of who we could become. If we stare long enough we cannot look away until that person is manifest, and we arrive at the inevitability that the greatest form of ourselves cannot be completed in a cage. We realize we must destroy the cage built around us. We must reclaim the right to our lives, our liberty, and the pursuit of happiness, and only then will we become truly American. Only then, will we be on the path of the American destiny.

Let it be known that the more you shake the chains of bondage the more you will be reviled. The more you rattle the cage the more you will be insulted, ridiculed, abused, beaten down, and humiliated. But rise like the sun. Always. And those who would shackle you won't even have the strength to look at you, for you will shine with such light that anyone who has a piece of America in their heart will gaze upon you like the star after which America is named, and be drawn to you, as our forefathers were drawn to this country, until all of America is united and her enemies scour the earth for sanctuary, only to find no darkness remains.

CHAPTER 3

# AMERICAN GREATNESS

Throughout history, no people achieved greatness through economics alone. In fact, economics has brought great empires to their ruin more often than it has propelled them to greatness, especially if leaned on in and of itself. A people died first when its culture was destroyed before they had been dominated; America itself did not become great through economics alone but through her values and her commitment to live in accordance with them.

A people that forgets its cultural identity and therefore how to live with integrity and in harmony with this cultural identity renders itself politically vulnerable to every influence imaginable. Those who stand for nothing fall for anything, and when there is no cultural square to perfect one's lifestyle they find themselves chasing economic gain alone at the expense of their moral character and cultural strength.

Leftism today means only globalism. In America, we have come to this conclusion, that more than 350 million people see America's outcome to be in the hands of a few leftist globalists. This has become possible only through the leftist influence on our culture, the globalization of every facet of our way of life. The undermining of the American conceptualizations of the American Dream, what it means to be American and our Manifest Destiny by buzzwords such as equity, democracy, equality, social justice, privilege, and patriarchy. These notions have eroded our culture like the ocean erodes a great stone: gradually and with such persistence as to inevitably render it to scattered grains of sand, never to come together as one great force again. Today we are forced to admit that even our weakest enemies have become stronger than America, for we cannot even win a war against the most primitive people who walk upon the face of the earth, be it in the jungle or in the desert. We are always forced to retreat in shame with years wasted, lives wasted, and trillions wasted.

No salvation is possible for America until those responsible for this erosion, the leftists, have been held responsible and made completely powerless to the point of no possible return, no possible further harm against America.

We must remember the protesters of January 6. It cannot be that hundreds of thousands of Americans should have come under the grip of the leftists in vain, and that afterward populist patriots are forced to come to the table with leftist traitors. We will never forget the 500 imprisoned or the 500,000 shamed, or the 350 million disenfranchised. We will not forgive, but we will avenge within the just means of the political process.

The dishonoring of Americans and consequently America must end once and for all, for traitors of their country belong in one state of living only—a state of powerlessness. Our cities will once again honor the names of American heroes whose statues have been torn down in the name of "progress." Our streets shall no longer be named after leftists, and in the question of who is responsible for the great decline of America, we must unashamedly and confidently proclaim the truth: leftists are responsible.

The state must be cleared of the traitors and foreign actors who have fattened themselves off of every individual American's accomplishments, and the two-party system must be shaken to the point of total collapse.

The relaxed attitude in which leaders of both the Political Right and the Political Left have chosen in response to the crippling of our people through inflationary measures, insurmountable debt, and social ostracization must be met with an overwhelming gavel of justice, as that would shake the knees of America's most wretched traitors.

We must demand America's second coming, an American renaissance—a new Enlightenment on the subject of who has negotiated American strength away for the sake of personal, political, and financial gain. We must awaken true Americans into a bottomless love for one another, affection for country, and animosity for those who have compromised her integrity.

We must bring an end to the lies which are designed to turn Americans against one another and inaccurately blame the wrong culprit for our present state of desperation. The fraud of the present political class must be revealed and it must awaken a new American conviction.

A new American currency backed by gold or hedged against inflation with blockchain technology must be established, and the leftists who have lived among us and brought our great America to this state of desperation must rectify their sins against their country by living a life stripped of political power in the face of a new America—an America never to be squandered again.

We must demand immediate expulsion of all leftists who have infested our political infrastructure, our parties, our schools, our institutions, our Sacred Senate, Holy House, and West Wing, who through their great deception have made themselves out to be our countrymen but have proven to be nothing but America's greatest enemy.

The housing crisis faced at first in our cities, which is now seeping into our rural communities, must be met with true American action! A temporary, if not permanent, eradication of all property tax must be enacted to afford true Americans the dignity of being able to afford their own home, or pay their own rent, without the state perpetuating a humiliating state of childhood by forcing Americans no alternative than to suckle at her breast.

Radical problems require radical solutions, and in order for us to overcome the infestation of leftism in our nation we must pull it out by the root and let it be met with the invisible hand of true capitalism once again; an economic system which brought America to her height of power is America's only hope for returning to her former glory. While the Left speaks of globalism, we must proclaim America First and Only America, for there is no better world than one in which America can be a shining beacon of light unto it.

In the populist patriots' view, the world was a better place and America a stronger nation before the existence of the World Economic Forum, NATO, the United Nations, and other globalist entities that have exploited America's great strength for their own globalist gains. The leftist pacifists proclaim that war is never necessary while simultaneously catalyzing conflict among any nation that would hold its sovereignty sacred. They proclaim that there is no need for conflict as they subject Americans to globalist trade agreements and other nations to globalist tribunals where their fate is determined by their very enemies without appeal.

History has proven that those who have not the strength to fight for themselves become the compromised subjects of those who would fight on their behalf or finally the subject of those whom they would fight against to no avail. Those who would proclaim "Peace is the only answer" fail to understand that peace can only be achieved through strength, for the history of the world has been a struggle to power, a struggle between the strong and the weak and the injustice created where these two collide.

In order for America to be at peace it must be strong, and in order for America to be strong it must be made of strong Americans. In order for globalism to prevail, America's sovereignty must be compromised, and her sovereignty can only be compromised if Americans themselves are brought to a state of weakness. A strong American base creates a strong American nation, which in turn can shield her people from globalist corruption and maintain the protection of individual rights among its own people within. Only this guarantee of protection within can catalyze the self-actualization of Americans themselves, and this strength can only be accomplished through uncompromising American strength culturally and militarily. We advocate not for interventionism, but the opposite! We advocate for the right not to be intervened with.

The conflict of interest between America and globalist entities can be found solely in the economic sphere. Up until recently, America's position as a world power was undisputed. Our economy was the strongest, our currency the strongest, our military the strongest, our intellects the brightest, our technology the most advanced. We were perceived as an insurmountable competitor—a nation that could not be conquered. We were not conquered, but we were corrupted through globalization and globalist agreements.

We imported Chinese Communist academics into our universities and showed them all of our technological advancements only to have them stolen and implemented by the Chinese Communist Party. We participated in international climate treaties where we contributed far more than our share and failed to hold our globalist neighbors accountable when they failed to contribute their fair share as originally agreed upon. We committed our military to the protection of European and Middle Eastern interests while our neighbors stood idly by as we threw our soldiers and our wealth into the bottomless abyss of unnecessary war.

Finally, we must ask ourselves: who benefits from a globalist America? For it seems to be everyone but Americans themselves.

The leftist political class continues to profit from these great conflicts, whether it is the military industrial complex supplying arms to our so called allies, or to our own military, which is coerced into constant conflict by special interests. Every natural disaster is met with unrivaled foreign aid where our political class personally benefits from the federal contracts supplying nations in need with food, water, electricity, and other infrastructure at the expense of the American people without actually solving the pathetic and vulnerable state of affairs anywhere.

The political class further weakens our borders to import labor into our country only for the wealth earned among this illegal class of immigrants to be sent back to their homeland without any remittance tax—and we wonder why our South American neighbors aren't doing their part to protect the sanctity of their borders? It is because their very economies rely on the invasion of labor into our lands and the raiding of our people like the Vikings raided and pillaged the shores of England long ago.

Our continued intervention in globalist affairs and the compromise of our own cultural integrity has amounted to no great affection for our people. Instead of thanks we are met with bitterness as our efforts made either out of goodwill or political corruption are perceived as patronizing, unjust, and heavy-handed. Not only has this hatred been directed against the government of the United States of America but against Americans themselves, where now the state of the world is such that an American cannot travel to any foreign land without being spit on, sneered at, or robbed.

For this reason, the leftist press of America has accomplished a masterful stroke of deception and convinced Americans that the only remedy is to continue in an unbridled attempt to sacrifice ourselves for the special interests of our globalist neighbors. Now, as a result, an inherently peace-loving people is brought to the brink of World War III by advocating for globalism against all national sovereignty, either foreign or domestic.

Who can prevent the next World War? The leftist press would have you believe it to be globalist intervention in national affairs, but what is a World War if not the epitome of a global intervention itself? There can be no world peace among nations subject to globalist interests.

Could Freemasonry rise again and stop the next World War just as they established our Great Revolution and the great liberation of France in the name of fraternity, equality, and liberty? The globalists have weakened even the Freemasons to the point of near extinction, where one cannot visit a Masonic lodge without gazing with sad eyes upon photographs of greater men taken generations ago.

Before 1971, when the dollar was backed by gold, America was the closest thing to a just capitalist nation capable of standing against leftism, but the international community became aware that we were spending more than we had backed in gold, and Nixon made the greatest error of his presidency and perhaps the greatest error of any president in the history of our nation—he removed the dollar from the gold standard and let loose the leash of leftism.

So, the leftists became revolutionaries, but to cripple America they did not take up arms but rather the printing press. Federal spending skyrocketed beyond the moon upon which we had landed just years before, and the value of our dollar has plummeted ever since regardless of which party has been in power. They disguised their aim to dismantle America as a great humanist movement in the name of "justice", "equality", "equity", "social justice", "welfare", and "human rights", to the point where today one cannot in seriousness call America sovereign for there is hardly a trace of America left to distinguish it from the globalist community.

Our leaders spend plenty of time abroad; even our governors travel abroad, leaving their states behind to ruin as they ask our foreign competitors, "What more can I give of my people to you that I might be compensated in return?" We see it every day in all aspects of our culture: the gluttony, debauchery, weakness, vigilantism, and mockery of working class Americans.

So, the great prophecy told for millennia by the fall of Rome is coming true in America today. The whole world has lashed out against us, and the private political press has even succeeded in turning us against ourselves, to the point where there is nothing left to live for but economic speculation and exploitation.

What guilt do true Americans bear for this other than the naivete that allowed them to trust those who would betray them? True Americans are not guilty of social injustice, patriarchy, bigotry, sexism, or racism. We are but guilty of one thing: that when our interests were sold to the globalists, that when our culture was shamed and our people turned against one another, that when our currency was weakened and our labor was outsourced to foreign communists, we did not stand up and say "No more."

But an American may yet rise up and ask the question, "Who has done this to our sacred country?" It is our great American duty to ask this question and, in pursuit of the answer, come to the inevitable conclusion that it is the leftist globalists among us who have compromised the political class and sold America to foreign special interests at great personal, political, and financial gain—all at the expense of the American people.

We have the duty to raise this question because soon will come the day when America reawakens and we take our nation back from those who have betrayed it. And when we have the gavel of justice clenched in our fists again we must render a just remedy upon the true culprit. When that day comes let it be known that despite their pleas there will have been no true change of heart among them. As today they are free to live among us, to deceive us into electing them into office and empowering them to sacrifice our people for corrupt global interests, so they must never be again.

Let us never forget while we have naively given the leftists the right and the power to betray us, we too, as true Americans, have our rights, and it is now our duty to reclaim them, and once reclaimed to keep them sacred and inviolable, so that every American can achieve a greatness never before seen. And America herself will once again become a light among men never to be dampened but only to be gazed upon with wonder, as all true Americans embark toward it only to find that God has blessed mankind with a second savior—not a man born of a virgin but a nation born of Americans.

CHAPTER 4

# THE AMERICAN CLASS

I reject the very notion that America is divided into two classes; that of the oppressor and the oppressed. The Marxist who created the very notion of oppressor versus oppressed has seeped into American culture and fattened his purse on the exploitation of dividing Americans against one another. This classification of Americans into either the class of the oppressor or the class of the oppressed has liberated those among us from the personal responsibility and culpability necessary to inspire them out of their present status and into one of hope and success. This state of things has empowered the leftists in America to exploit the plight of the most vulnerable Americans, to further their plight and thus their political power with it.

And while the leftist organizes the "oppressed" masses, he capitalizes on their suffering at the same time either by wielding these masses for political power or exploiting them for financial gain by new industries centered around diversity, equity, and inclusion at the expense of true justice and at great harm to our American nature, which is naturally averse to racism but is embracing that sin once again in the name of equity.

Consequently, American business has lost the American values of hard work, accomplishment, and accountability and ventured into the postmodern realm of subjective values and immeasurable outcomes.

Ultimately, the leftists who created this class division among the oppressor and the oppressed are the same who led the masses in the opposition to this very division, led them not against the leftist ideals which have created this dynamic of injustice but led them against the false enemy of their successful American neighbors, business owners, intellectuals, and others.

This caused the remaining American business culture to resist the masses whom they found at the gate demanding better conditions. As the mob grew larger and larger, so did the concessions among American industry, and as the concessions grew the leftists proclaimed "See! Their actions are an admission of guilt. Your struggle is their undoing." If it had not been for the endless complacency and greed among leaders of American industry, the leftist would never have become the leader of the American working class. Millions of our fellow Americans would never have been alienated from one another based on wealth and success had it not been for the political class of our nation failing to show any genuine care for the welfare of our people, who instead feigned compassion as it was politically prudent to do so despite its deeply immoral deception.

It's time for Americans to admit to themselves that the political party of the Right is not the savior we hoped it was and will not lead us to the promised land of liberty. Our parties lack the will of conviction, the courage of heroes, and the energy of youth to take on the necessary task before them. Where then can this strength be found within America? It must be found where it always was—in the masses of the American people who have been unconsciously awaiting an awakening to the call: "The time is now to fight for your country."

This fight alone can liberate the American people from the shackles of leftism, and true Americans must answer the call and swell up like a great wave upon the shore and saturate America with an overwhelming force of unity and inspiration. Without the help of working class

Americans and business class Americans alike, America's second coming cannot be actualized.

The strength of our nation does not rest on the power of her political parties but in the hearts, minds, and hands of the American people. It is true today as it has always been true that liberation does not come from above but from the people themselves who have the courage and conviction to live up to that divine promise of life, liberty, and the pursuit of happiness. If we can this day make the highest demand of every true American, then every true American will demand the freedom from and respect of the entire world.

The Political Right has lost all energy; they see the flood coming as the Political Left flees their posts in the form of mass political resignation. Their long forgotten longing for a strong America has been rendered moot by their abundant incompetence. Such is the state of all our political leaders either on the Right or Left—nowhere to be found when America needs American heroes not political grandstanders.

On the Left we see somewhat more energy, but that energy is used to further the exploitation of the American people, not to render a more just and fair state of things for them. The leftists preach love of the Democratic Party over love of country, and they saddle themselves in political bureaucracy rather than practical solutions for a suffering people.

Yet, both the Political Right and the Political Left know it to be true that an enemy is arising among the people and for that they are terrified as the masses are unifying against those who have told only lies and enacted only exploitation. This new movement will ultimately produce a fanatic Americanism that will become an unstoppable force.

What populist patriots want is not an America of drones such as we saw during the pandemic, quietly walking by with their masks over their faces in fear, their concerns silenced amid censorship, and their liberty compromised in the face of a state they misguidedly felt too strong to stand against. We want an America that protects the right for everyone to keep for themselves that which they have earned, the right to own. An America that embraces honest work. An America that cares not for the interests of foreign nations but for the interests of its own people.

Therefore, America must not become dependent on globalist regulation. If anyone believes that globalism cannot be avoided let him see with his own eyes as America establishes national sovereignty again. Finally, the greatest injustice which has befallen our American people must be corrected, and such unity among the American people must be reached so as to clean our institutions of the leftist infestation that has rendered her prey to all those who have and will continue to exploit her, both foreign and domestic.

What we need if we are to have a truly Populist America is a true immigration reform: the strengthening of our borders and the allowance of citizenship only to be awarded to those who bring value to America rather than weakening it in the face of the globalist threat— for we cannot claim to be a nation if we do not have borders, and we cannot claim to be a great ship if we are constantly taking on water.

Further, we must protect the private property rights of all Americans, for we cannot claim to be a sovereign nation if we do not respect the sovereignty of the American people on their own property, who produce their own wealth through the work of their hands, and build our great America with all that they accomplish within it.

Additionally, we must reform our laws not only to protect the rights of individuals but to protect the very values of Americanism: the protection of our people, our community, and our culture. Our education needs to be reformed so that we cease to suffer the cultural degradation resulting from the leftism that has infested the childhood of our precious youth. We have lost our American instinct by confusing our youth's understanding of American culture—by degrading the appreciation of it and consequently weakening the integrity of American life.

We have a highly capable intellectual class in America, but it has no courage, and when it has courage it has no clarity of action to enact true change. We need a true restoration to an intellectual integrity that put us on the moon or connected the entire world with the great technological advancement that was the Internet itself. If the intellectuals within America had not allowed Marxist leftists to infest our educational institutions, we would not have found ourselves forgetting who we are, but would have doubled down on American values and accomplished far more than we have seen from America the past many decades. What we need is the continuous succession of intellectuals teaching and thinking in harmony with American ideals drawn from the true American people and the values by which they live.

Vanquish leftism from our institutions! The American people are genius enough and we have no need for leftist ideals, confusion, or stupidity to distract our great minds away from the work before them. If we had not allowed our intellectuals to be distracted with leftist ideas and shamed by leftist principles of oppressor versus oppressed, imagine how much further our American Mind would have advanced.

## We Need a Reform of the American Press

Our press has become fundamentally anti-American, for it has violated the sacred principle of truth by telling only lies, the sacred value of integrity by covering for the corrupt, and the sacred notion of patriotism by shaming Americans for any virtue they have harbored, be it personal success, liberty, strength, or enterprise. We must hold the press accountable when it lies and afford it every protection when it broadcasts the truth despite any opposition against it.

We must see to it that our people are not poisoned by globalist cultural imposition. We must see to it that our entertainment is not compromised by communist ideals in pursuit of reaching greater global markets but that artists can make the art in their hearts, authors can write the literature from their own pen, and creators can manifest that which they have envisioned without the compromise of third parties who, having not the proper reverence for the sacred creation of a creator, have malformed the creative authenticity of America.

After these reforms we shall realize the duty of every American individual. An American who denies himself the right to defend his life and liberty has denied the right of his neighbor to defend his life and liberty, and has therefore disregarded the very right for America itself to exist at all. This lack of American conviction, of American character, renders all who live it unfit to call themselves American.

Therefore we populist patriots advocate for the Second Amendment and the ownership and training with arms of all true Americans, regardless of their immutable characteristics. If you believe that you are free, then you must believe that you have the right, even the duty, to defend that freedom not only for yourself but for your fellow Americans as well.

What Americans need are not leaders in Congress but those among us who are willing to live according to the rights that have been bestowed upon us at birth by God Himself. If we find success in raising such Americans from our people to lead us beyond the two-party deception, then America herself will spontaneously reform and the American patriotism that manifests before us will awaken every American with a semblance of love for life, liberty, and the pursuit of happiness in his heart to rise up to injustice and say, "No more!"

Let every American remember that the Fourth of July is not a day separate from every day in the year, but a day that proclaims that every day in America should be filled with liberty and independence from global interests. Whatever virtue that America ever had did not come out of globalism but from within, from the very soul of the American people. When Americans have lost their creative force, then they become leftists; wherever their intellectual capacity is abandoned, they become leftists; and there is no wonder that those among us who advocate for American globalism are those in the political class—a class of people who cannot create, think, or produce on their own but merely exploit the creations of others, the production of others, and that which was never theirs to begin with.

So each American day should only be lived to glorify the American will over globalist erosion, of the liberation of the American people from the shackles of despotism toward an independent and thriving capitalism. So, the question we must ask ourselves is: "Will America see another spring, or are we stuck in perpetual winter, where our very soul seems dormant without hope of awakening?" And this question is where populist patriotism begins.

There are three principles upon which this movement rests its hope for America's second coming: American populism, American individualism, and American patriotism. Populism is the love of the American people. Individualism is the recognition that the American people are composed of individuals, and therefore the American people prosper when the rights of every individual are protected. Patriotism is our willingness to live in accordance with that love. We know only one interest, and that is the interest of the American people. Of America First. Of only America.

Populist patriots are radical in their love for the American people, and we are committed to establishing the political power necessary to make the government recognize and embody that love itself. We are abundantly loyal to our fellow Americans and fanatically opposed to those among us who would for a moment take and use our love of country to gain power through us, only to turn and exploit us once power has been attained. We do not waste time on those who compromise, on moderates, on political leaders who pull us Left or who pull us Right, for we see only one way forward for America, not forward but upward!

Populist patriots have faith in the American people and in their quality of character to live good lives in accordance with a greater degree of liberty and the protection of their rights. We focus not on the injustices committed on foreign people by foreign nations but on the assurance that no injustice should befall the American people in service to any globalist interest. We must make it abundantly known among all true Americans that our sacred sovereignty and the sovereignty of our people can only be regained and preserved with an uncompromising commitment to America, and can never be actualized by voting for the lesser of two evils but by thoroughly removing corruption from every corner of our country, wherever it can be found.

When others doubt or hesitate about America's future, we have total faith; we have the hope and faith that a day will come when America reawakens and consequently is reborn. We have faith that God will look upon America once again and smile upon her as a nation set apart, and on this Independence Day will truly have come.

CHAPTER 5

# OVERCOMING DEMOCRACY

---

There are two things that history proves are capable of bringing people together. The first is common idealism, and the second is a common conspiracy to commit crimes. If America's second coming isn't brought on the back of idealism, then it will come in the form of the greatest crime in our history. Populist patriots realize that from the infamous globalist cesspool of corrupt conspiracy, nothing can come but harm to America.

We know that two things alone will save us. First, the end of globalist corruption and exploitation of America, and the cleansing of those members of the political class who owe their status to perpetuating this exploitation. Only the most ruthless and unforgiving account of our political class, the bringing of these leftists to justice and the eradication of them from our institutions once and for all will allow the restoration of our great nation.

Second, there must be an American government with the courage to declare foreign interests not in the interest of America, and the terms of our globalist agreements need to be totally abandoned in favor of total renegotiation. Then we will see if the globalist political class can turn 350 million Americans into their subjects.

If cowards cry out, "But we have no manufacturing of our own!" that is but a small challenge in the face of the alternative total subjugation of our nation to the will of globalist elites. When the whole of the American people knows one will and one will alone—to be free—in that very moment we will have the instrument with which to win our freedom: the will of the people. Any American who looks into the eyes of an American child can see that the challenge ahead of liberating America from global dependence is but small in the face of the ever-growing despair our people face and the doom for which we leave our children no alternative.

Today we know that America is one third heroic, one third cowardly, and one third traitors. As a condition of our freedom in respect to the globalist interests and the interests of the exploitative political class, we would first cleanse our domestic leadership of any leadership lacking in the courage or conviction to make right what has been so wronged.

The present two-party system has failed in that effort, for what was meant to be a dynamic system of accountability manifested in a single-party system of deception and conspiracy.

There must be an American reckoning for those who for years have led us into their criminal exploitation. The domestic fight must come before America can stand a chance in the face of the globalist threat to our national sovereignty. The reckoning will come when those who say "We are proud to be American" cease evading those who are effectively American in name only and force those without principle to yield to those who have it. The populist patriot movement is opposed by the leftist political class who cry, "Our democracy is in danger!" Their democracy is indeed in danger, and how long do they think they can maintain such an anti-American state of things?

Populist patriotism has manifested organically without any election in mind but with only the salvation of our country in mind. The task of the America First movement is not to prepare ourselves for any election for the House, the Senate, or the West Wing, but to prepare for the coming collapse of America itself, so that when the fall of this faux

American Empire inevitably presents itself, populist patriotism will remain standing.

We are the supporters of a second American coming, a rule by populist reason, of populist energy, of American conviction. America can be saved only through action, when through our movement the blindfold is stripped from the eyes of every American. It is from our movement that redemption will come to America—this today is the sentiment of millions of Americans, and they are adopting a new patriotic zeal with an almost religious fanaticism of faith, with only one of two possible outcomes: the total rebirth of America or her total and permanent collapse.

A leftist America and a patriotic America cannot much longer exist side by side, and the greatest influence to fall upon the face of our country will be that movement that promises and convinces the American people of an American renaissance. Either America collapses and we, through our cowardice, collapse with it, or we step into the new frontier as true Americans to build a new world founded upon a renewed commitment to American ideals. Then, we shall see whether the strength of America can overcome the evil of globalism.

This American republic was founded to be a nation of the American people, but through leftist and globalist ideals, through corruption and deception, has become a faux democracy designed only to secure the political power of the political class and amass great swaths of wealth for domestic and foreign globalist peers alike.

Long has it been since there has been given any thought to establishing or maintaining a state to represent the interests of the American people. The object has been to provide a leftist mob consisting of the most compromised and corrupt individuals with an object for their exploitation. A mob who itself has never worked; and if we refuse to acknowledge these facts, the globalist political class will continue their exploitation, for they are intimately familiar with the true nature of our political climate.

Hardly was the first deed of America's betrayal—the advent of the Federal Reserve—completed before another betrayal was committed, and another, and another, until all Americans are left with is a list of betrayals committed by those sworn to protect the people from such corruption.

Our political class can be seen visiting leaders all over the globe, entering restaurants most Americans would only dream of being able to afford, spas, hotels, resorts, mansions, yachts. They serve America's enemies in order to perpetuate the standard of living they have come to be accustomed to. The name *political swamp* will remain with them for as long as history is to be recorded.

Our nation was founded through the personality of brilliant leaders and by a people courageous enough to ensure their rights would never be violated again. Compare our founding heroes with the likes of our current political class for a moment and you'll realize that the America of 1776 is not the United States of today—the United States which sends our troops to die then leaves them behind on the battlefield, who taxes working class Americans and deflates their currency in order to launder it through corrupt institutions and foreign programs. The present day political leaders have dishonored all those who have ever fought for America!

Hardly has there ever been a period of five or ten years where more has been torn away from the American people and given to our foreign neighbors or directly to the pockets of our very own political class. We have been rendered defenseless against our foreign enemies with the weakening of our nation's military, and our American people have been left defenseless in the face of a corrupt political class that can persecute true Americans without recourse due to the erosion of the constitutional protection of our rights.

The leftists have made three changes in our state that have brought us to the pinnacle of corruption today: they have globalized our domestic policies, globalized the strength of our currency, and globalized the culture of the American people itself, thereby globalizing every individual American among us. While the American people were told lies about the globalization of America it was globalized right before their very eyes by the corrupt exploitation of the people, without their consent, by the political class.

Through this globalization, Americans have ceased to be the masters of their own fate and now have been rendered subjects of the globalist fief. Is this the America our American heroes imagined? No. It is a leftist paradise.

When did the ruin of America begin? When the political class sought to become the world's police while simultaneously seeking the economic conquest of the world. These two principles cannot maintain the strength of a people, for no nation can fight a war on two fronts, manifest a conflict of interest within itself, and seek to accomplish the self-actualization of its destiny.

What then has the state become as a result of this? Today it is an economic organization run by the political class for the continued exploitation of the American people in exchange for providing insufficient welfare for the people. The state was never meant to be an economic organization; it was not meant to regulate business, outsource the production of fiat currency, or be involved in the daily business of our private institutions to such an extent that fascism prevails.

The purpose of the state is to protect the sovereignty of the people. To protect the borders from outside violations of the rights of her people and to protect the individuals within from the violation of rights by the mob. But our state has become something that protects not the borders, enforces not the rule of law among the people, and not only fails to protect the rights of the people, but violates those rights itself.

If today the populist patriotism movement is thought among circles in America as being inherently hostile to the United States, let me first say: *It is hostile to the corrupt political class as all great American movements have been and should be, and what is more hostile against the American people than the government of the United States itself?*

I regard it as of the utmost importance for Americans to break with all of those members of the political class and their constituents who view our American destiny as intertwined with world events. It is not true that the cause of our distress has been entirely domestic or that the solution to global problems must therefore be a globalist America—our problems are due to the mistakes made by the political class and the complacency of the American people to stand idly by and allow these mistakes to be continuously made. The state of things in America today is due to the work of men who did not have our best interests at heart, and the complacency of men convinced wrongfully of their inability to stand up and do something about it. But Americans will awaken to this lie and those responsible for America's managed decline will be held accountable.

It is a terrible lie to say that our lives in America today are solely determined by the considerations of globalist interests or that our political class today is destined to exploit our domestic life to the globalist ideal, for as long as there is breath in our lungs there is hope for an America reborn.

It is false for us to say that the globalist forces are solely responsible for the American demise, for the globalists are doing what is in their nature—exploiting that which can be exploited—and therefore the fault is on our own leaders for allowing us to be exploited, for allowing themselves to be compromised, for betraying the very American people they have sworn to protect. It is a problem made in America and it is a problem that can only be corrected in America.

There is a factor which historically has culminated in a nation's decline: that the value of a nation's personality and those individuals within it are gradually eroded by the notion of the supremacy of numbers—the fallacy that that which is most popular is most true. Thus we have the blossoming of democratic ideals that supersede the value of individual rights and individual accomplishment, even going so far as to hold those individuals who are most successful to be most culpable for a nation's distress.

Globalism and democracy are inseparable because all democracy leads to leftism and all leftism leads to globalism, for leftism is not a self-sustaining political philosophy but one of exploitation and therefore has to expand beyond its borders until finally there is nothing left to exploit.

Democracy denies the value of the individual and replaces it with the value of the masses as a whole. Of course, this position is unsustainable, for one cannot advocate properly for the masses without acknowledging that the people themselves are composed at their very core of individuals, and therefore to subvert the individual is to compromise the masses.

By subverting the individual in favor of the mob, democracy dismisses the value of the individual, their rights, and ultimately their property as nothing sacred to a person but something the masses are inherently entitled to instead. This philosophy that recognizes nothing extraordinary or different among individuals is destined for injustice as it holds all individuals to be exactly congruent in value, but they are not—for some among us are extraordinary and our intelligence, talent, and contribution to society is not equal. Naturally, every special talent and every fundamental value of a people is rendered practically inconsequential and snuffed out by the mob itself, for the greatness of a people is the result not of the sum of its achievement but the sum of its *outstanding* achievements—achievements that cannot manifest without the self-actualization of extraordinary individuals. So it stands to reason that a society founded on the disregard for the extraordinary individuals is a society incapable of extraordinary accomplishment. For this reason democracy never manifests in the rule of the people but in reality the rule of the average, the midwits, the ordinary.

Consequently, true democracy can only lead to the destruction of a great people and their authentic personality—their authentic values. This explains why the more leftist a people becomes, the more democratic, the less extraordinary they become as well. We saw this with the advent of the Soviet Union; we've seen this in China, North Korea, and other Marxist nations that have transitioned from great human achievement to the endeavor of mimicking the achievements of others. How many communist pianists can play Beethoven perfectly? Hundreds and thousands! But how many communist composers can you name who write with the authority of Beethoven, Mozart, Rachmaninoff, or others?

Democracy inherently leads to a people's entropy and their entropy naturally catalyzes tyranny. Therefore we must admit that the leading cause of tyranny is democracy itself, and America must never fall into the clutches of the mob but must hold the rights of each individual American sacred and inviolable. Let us be a nation of unequal prosperity and not one of equal poverty. Let us be a nation that celebrates the accomplishments of extraordinary individuals instead of one that resents their success with a bitter lack of self-esteem. Allow yourselves the right to become your best selves and the courage to embrace the accomplishments of others, for there can be no self-actualization without individual freedom and there cannot be a Great America without Americans achieving greatness. We are equal under the law, but not equal in the paths that destiny has laid before us. We each have our own paths of various outcomes, but we share one American path—the path toward American greatness.

CHAPTER 6

# AMERICA'S HOLY TRINITY

From the earliest memories of our childhood we can recall having dreams for what the future would entail for us. We are born with the inherent belief that there is something truly special about us that we can bring to the world to make lasting change—that we can touch the lives of those around us and actualize our greatest potential. For many Americans, these dreams dim as we grow older and are faced with the obstacles of life. What once seemed within reach now seems impossible by the debt we are saddled with, the upward mobility in our careers that is nowhere to be found, and the burden of necessity that comes to be a priority over the vision for ourselves that is ideal.

This self-actualization has not yet been rendered impossible by leftist policies in America, but Americans have been rendered hopeless out of the cultural impact that we have allowed leftists to have on our morale. We are told that the world is divided into the oppressor versus the oppressed and that our status in life is a product of our environment rather than how we respond to it. We are told that if we are poor it is because we are the victims of injustice and there is nothing we can do to overcome adversity but demand that those who have achieved power and success be brought to justice.

This constant saturation of doubt and hopelessness has rendered Americans not only to a point of losing all faith in our great country, but to losing all faith in themselves. We look around and see the powerful and the powerless and forget the sacred truth that no matter the external circumstances, we can still seize complete power over self.

Self-actualization is the manifestation of an individual's full potential. It is achieved only when we meet our physiological needs, our safety needs, a sense of love and belonging, and finally self-esteem. The leftist movement has rendered self-actualization nearly impossible by making the basic necessities more and more difficult to attain through the inflation of our dollar and the increased dependence on the state.

Leftism has made our communities more dangerous so that we are in constant increased fear of personal security through the disarmament of our urban citizens. They weakened our sense of job security by continuously disrupting the economy and inserting "wokeism" in the workplace, and they restricted the production of American resources in the name of environmentalism. They made access to healthcare more difficult through sweeping healthcare reforms, and made property so expensive as to be nearly impossible to afford through property tax and an artificial reduction in the housing supply by decreasing the efficiency of the supply chain and inflating the cost of domestic labor.

The Left has directly attacked our individual American sense of love and belonging by shaming the patriotism out of the hearts of our children, dividing us by race and class, and making us to feel inherently evil by virtue of the very land we occupy—calling us colonizers, privileged, bigoted, and merely outcomes of the patriarchy.

They have crippled our sense of self-esteem by convincing us that the individual is merely an entity meant for sacrifice to the greater good, to the collectivist whole, to the community, to the masses, the mob. They have convinced us that all that is good about us is a product of privilege and that nothing we accomplish is our own to proudly claim.

For every American, this can end in a moment. The moment he or she realizes the lie of the leftist. If one American has the audacity to deny the great lie that is instilled in our culture by the neo-leftists, then this American can immediately free himself of the shackles of shame.

The leftist tends to hate anything that appears to be good, strong, or successful. They hate America and virtually all aspects of Western civilization including logic, reason, and even science itself. They say they hate these things because of the West's history of injustice, but in reality all of the Marxist nations have exhibited the vices of Western civilization tenfold, and so this cannot be the real reason for the leftist's hate of America and the American individual. The real hate for America is because it has been strong, and their bitterness is the manifestation of their deep insecurity and lack of self-esteem.

The leftist does not believe in self-esteem but collective sensitivity; they do not believe in self-reliance but social safety nets; not in optimism but in hopelessness; and they cannot fathom the individual finding strength from within for they have relied on external sources for their own sense of worth for so long that the notion strength can be found within is utterly offensive to them, as it implies their entire worldview is the inversion of reality itself and therefore unsustainable. Their shame being boundless, they cannot tolerate anything that directs their vision inward, for they know they have nothing within but an abyss of self-hatred. And so, they hate you so they don't have to hate themselves.

Contemporary leftists focus on abstract art because objective reality is something they find deeply offensive. Their philosophies dismiss objective reality and personal accountability—for the leftist everything must be relative, for if all reality is subjective then they never have to face the reality of their own wretchedness, let alone put in the work to rectify it (this work being the very human condition itself, which they utterly deny).

The leftist's arguments are based on emotional feeling instead of rational thought, for they are guided by what provides them with the greatest sense of self-righteousness and moral superiority rather than what would unmistakably be found to be true should they follow the curiosity of their minds over the emotional needs of their selflessness—that they have failed themselves and through that failure they have failed their country and all of mankind itself.

The leftist can never reach self-actualization, for the leftist fails the first step, which is the knowing of self. For the leftist, knowing oneself is the most terrifying of endeavors, so instead of looking inward to discover his own soul, the leftist looks outward to define himself relative to the rest of society. This is why the leftist is often lost, unfulfilled, lonely, and bitter and the only immediate alleviation the leftist gets from their anguish is to offload it on everyone he interacts with. The greatest ecstasy the leftist can attain is that of enacting policy that enforces this anguish upon the greatest number of people possible.

To the extent that the leftist is empowered, the individual American's ability to self-actualize is inhibited, for self-actualization requires freedom. One cannot become the best version of oneself without the freedom to live according to one's true nature.

Freedom is the power to have control over the circumstances that determine one's life. The freedom to live where and how one wants to live, to obtain through work the necessities of life without the supervision of others—to clothe oneself and feed oneself, to shelter oneself and work for oneself. The degree to which the aspects of human life are controlled by leftist regulation is inversely correlated to the degree in which an individual can be free in that environment. Consequently, leftism is a violation of every individual's rights who lives under leftist influence.

The leftist has attempted to move America's emphasis on individual rights to collective rights. The beginning of this was seen among the labor unions, and the manifestation of it today can be found in the rampant use of identity politics. Since only an individual can possess rights, the notion of individual rights is inherently redundant, and the notion of collectivist rights inherently absurd.

A group or community can have no rights other than the rights of its individual members, just as a group cannot be a group without the individual members within it. In a truly free society the rights of any group are synonymous with the rights the individuals within that group possess. The individuals do not get their rights from the group, but the group gets its rights from the individuals within it!

Just as a person cannot attain new rights by joining a group or lose his rights by leaving one, the moral principle of a truly free society must be the advocacy of individual rights regardless of group identity. Inherently, the notion of group rights implies that rights belong to some groups and not others, which is antithetical to the American notion of inherent individual rights.

Therefore, individual rights cannot be the subject of a vote— something our forefathers understood, and why America was designed to be a constitutional republic and not a democracy. The individual's rights *must* be protected against the whim of the mob, otherwise the degradation of American culture, prosperity, and strength will continue its exponential trajectory toward collapse.

So what are American individuals to do in the face of this leftist violation of their individual rights? First, Americans must reclaim their individual sovereignty and adopt the principle that self-esteem must be found from within, that our failures are our own, and that though we may never be perfect, we can always be better.

Once Americans have reclaimed self-ownership they can begin the process of self-knowing, which ultimately guides each individual toward their own personal fulfillment. As we begin to live in accordance with our values and with integrity to our individual identities we will meet countless instances of adversity. Face the ridicule, criticism, pushback, and abuse with courage, and wear the leftist attacks against you like a badge of honor! For if in the face of adversity you have chosen the easy concession to leftist harassment over your own integrity, you have not only betrayed yourself but you have betrayed your country.

We cannot always choose the circumstances we are in or the environment that surrounds us, but we can always choose how we respond to it. This is the ultimate truth of individual sovereignty that the Left cannot take from you without consent. If every American refuses to compromise their very self to the whims of the mob, then America with be organically reborn through the very individuals within it who deny the mob any jurisdiction over their own life, liberty, or pursuit of happiness. Reclaim your life and you will have reclaimed your country.

Simply put, American actualization is an America that reaches the total potential of its people. Consequently, that capacity can only be reached by the uniform self-actualization of every individual within America. This, of course, is likely impossible, for no individual can be perfect and consequently no group of individuals can reach perfection itself, but America can drastically improve her proximity to its ideal form, closer than we have reached today or at any moment in the past.

The question then becomes not what America must do as a nation but what America must be to her people so that they may achieve the greatest possible closeness to their own actualization.

A government is simply a monopoly on physical force. This force can be used for the just protection of rights or the immoral violation of rights, but when all is said and done a government's power can be reduced to their ability to physically force a desired behavior or outcome.

Since every individual is born equipped with a mind, and a mind is nature's gift to man to be used for his own survival and prosperity, then the first function of a government is to protect the right to free thought and speech, for without it no man can attain self-actualization.

Not only must a person be able to think and speak freely, but he must be able to act in accordance with his reason—to live according to his values so long as his actions do not infringe upon the rights of others. Naturally, that which a man thinks is his own thought, that which he says is his own speech, and that which he does is his own action—therefore, that which he produces with his thought, speech, and work is his property and no one else's.

A government that robs an individual of his right to think, speak, and act and ultimately robs that individual of the product of his work or attempts to regulate his thoughts and actions is not a just government but an organized mob.

A man's right to his own life necessitates a man's right to defend himself against the violence of others, and consequently a nation that purports to protect the rights of its people must be willing to defend its people against violent aggression from enemies both foreign and domestic. A government's role is merely to enforce objective and rational laws enacted for the protection of individual rights and the common defense of a people within its borders.

Since the protection of individual rights is the sole purpose of a just government, the protection of individual rights is the only just aim of any piece of legislation—all other laws are an overstep and a violation of the rights of the people a government is empowered to protect.

Therefore the only just role of government can be divided into three parts: the police, to protect individuals from criminals; the military, to protect people from foreign aggression; and a judiciary, to enforce the contractual agreements made between individual members of a society.

An actualized America is one with a government that without exception carries out these three duties while doing as little else as possible. We have forgotten that our Constitution is not meant to be a limit on individual Americans, but is itself a limit on the government alone. It is meant to keep the federal government from indefinite expansion, and ultimately it has failed in that effort despite its many remarkable accomplishments.

We have an American government today that regulates virtually every business, fails to enforce contracts, neglects the right to a fair and speedy trial, spends trillions, and has created a department for virtually every aspect of our society. The government has eked its way into our education via the Department of Education and inflated the cost of tuition by lending students inordinate amounts of money. We have healthcare legislation that has dramatically increased the cost of care, housing regulation that has increased the cost of housing, and an outsourced and unconstitutional monetary system that leaves the value of our currency to the whim of private centralized banking interests.

A dramatic reduction in federal spending is the only hope for the American dollar, and this dramatic reduction in spending can be accomplished only by a radical commitment to our government's reduction to its fundamental intended purpose. The less the government does, the greater our people will become—the less regulated our economy becomes, the more socio-economic justice will manifest among us.

But what does the manifestation of this minimalist approach to government look like? It is the catalyzation of traditional American values.

An America that focuses not on the safety of its people from the natural obstacles of life but instead focuses on the freedom of individuals to respond accordingly with their own reason and will to those challenges is an America that values individual industriousness.

An America that focuses not on an overreaching government that involves itself in every aspect of American life is an America that values personal responsibility and accountability.

An America that focuses not on enriching the political class through federal contracts and foreign interventionism is an America that esteems the honest accomplishment of individuals rather than regarding it with bitter resentment.

An America that involves itself not in the cultural indoctrination of its people is an America that values independent thought and self-esteem.

An America that involves itself not with globalist interests is an America that values individual sovereignty, and as a result its people will reach far greater achievements than those of even the most impressive among us today.

* * *

The most tenable outcome of such an America and such an American people will be a renaissance of American patriotism. Such greatness will America achieve that all who prosper within it will adore it for the world will look upon America again with envy.

It is through a love of the American people that we must commit ourselves to a love of self, for through our own self-actualization we do a greater service to the American people than anything else that is possible under the sun. Through this love of self we create a people worthy of love, and the American people demand the adoration of any rational person. Further, through the American protection of and adoration for the individual American we empower every individual to achieve greatness, and thus through the reciprocity of love for the people by the individual and love for the individual by the people, we create a cycle of American greatness.

It is through patriotism that we can become our best selves, and through becoming our best selves that we become patriots. An American cannot claim to love oneself and hate the American people, for every American is the American people and the American people cannot claim to love their country yet hate the American individual, for the nation itself is the American individual.

Consequently the American individual, the American populist, and the American patriot are the Holy Trinity of Americanism itself, for one cannot exist with integrity without the other two, and they are separate, equal, and one all in the same.

Thus it is your duty as an American to love yourself, and to love your people, and to live according to the principles of that love.

## Chapter 7

# A GREATER PEOPLE

---

In times of great turmoil and uncertainty, a nation stands at the crossroads of destiny, where the paths of despair and greatness diverge. Our beloved country, rich in heritage and steeped in the valor of our forebears, now faces challenges that threaten to unravel the very fabric of our society. The specters of economic devastation, seen in the harrowing depths of the Great Depression, the stark despair of the Great Recession, and the unyielding grip of a global pandemic, have cast long shadows over our land.

Yet, in the midst of these trials, there emerges a clarion call for change—a call that resonates in the hearts of the true sons and daughters of this great nation. It is not merely a call for superficial reform or fleeting political victories. No, this is a call for a profound transformation of our political landscape, a reawakening of the spirit that once made our nation unparalleled in its greatness.

For too long, the machinations of a disconnected and self-serving political elite have steered our country away from its true course. The two-party system, a duopoly of power, has proven inadequate, ensnared in perpetual conflict and partisan gridlock, failing to address the cries of the common man. Likewise, the insidious tendrils of globalism have sought to dilute our national identity, to erode the sovereignty that is our birthright.

In this pivotal moment, we stand on the brink of a new era—an era where the voice of the people echoes in the halls of power, where our shared struggles and triumphs rekindle a sense of national unity. It is time for a new movement, one that transcends the old paradigms of Left and Right, one that embodies the indomitable will and enduring values of our people.

This movement of American populism is manifesting One American Party. It's not just a political entity, but a beacon of hope, a testament to the resilience and strength of our nation. It is a rallying cry for all who envision a future where our country reclaims its rightful place as a bastion of freedom, prosperity, and unwavering spirit.

Let us not forget that this is not the first moment of desperation in our nation's history. In the annals of our nation's history, there are chapters written in the somber ink of hardship and despair. Times of economic calamity have not just been mere footnotes; they have been seismic events that shook the very foundations of our society, molding the character of our people and the destiny of our nation.

The Great Depression, a dark era that descended like a plague in the aftermath of the Roaring Twenties, serves as a stark reminder of the fragility of economic prosperity. It was a time when the roaring engines of industry fell silent, when breadlines stretched like the shadows of a setting sun, and the American Dream seemed but a fleeting whisper in the cold winds of poverty. This was not merely an economic downturn; it was a national crisis that called into question the very principles upon which our economy was built.

Emerging from the ashes of the Great Depression, our nation faced yet another formidable challenge with the Great Recession. Like a storm that comes unbidden, it ravaged our shores, leaving in its wake a trail of unemployment, lost homes, and shattered lives. The pillars of finance and industry, once thought unassailable, trembled under the weight of their own hubris. It was a vivid demonstration of the inherent flaws in our economic system, a system that favored the few at the expense of the many.

And then came the pandemic, an invisible enemy that brought the world to its knees. It was a global crisis that transcended borders, yet its impact was deeply personal, felt in every home, every heart. The pandemic was more than a health crisis; it was a mirror reflecting our vulnerabilities, exposing the shortcomings of our preparedness, our healthcare system, and our ability to stand united in the face of adversity.

These crises are not isolated incidents; they are interconnected chapters in a saga of economic vulnerability. Each one has chipped away at the facade of stability and prosperity, revealing a harsh truth: our nation has been walking a tightrope, with the safety net of economic security frayed and worn.

But in these moments of trial, there lies a profound opportunity— an opportunity for introspection, for learning, and for rebirth. We must look back at these events not just to lament, but to learn. We must understand the causes of these crises, recognize the failures of leadership and policy that allowed them to fester, and vow never to repeat the mistakes of the past.

It is through the lens of history that we can truly comprehend the magnitude of our current challenges and the urgency with which we must act. These economic hardships have been a crucible, testing the mettle of the American people. Yet, each time, we have emerged stronger, more resilient, more united in our resolve to build a better future.

In our pursuit of a brighter future, we must first confront the stark realities of our present circumstances. The systems that govern our great nation, once the heralds of progress, have become ensnared in a web of inefficiency and disconnection from the very people they are meant to serve. It is a tale of two grave maladies that afflict our political body: the pervasive influence of globalism and the inherent limitations of the two-party system.

Globalism, with its siren song of international cooperation and economic integration, has seduced many leaders away from the true interests of the nation. It promised prosperity and peace but delivered dependence and dilution of our cherished values and identity. Under the guise of global interconnectedness, we have seen the erosion of our sovereignty, the outsourcing of our jobs, and the weakening of our economic fortitude. The globalist agenda has not been the rising tide that lifts all boats, but rather a storm that has left many of our citizens adrift in a sea of uncertainty and despair.

Equally troubling is the two-party system, a duopoly that has dominated our political landscape for far too long. This system, deeply entrenched in the halls of power, has fostered an environment of partisanship and division. It has become a theater of endless conflict, where the pursuit of power often overshadows the pursuit of the public good. The two-party system has led to a political stagnation, where meaningful change is often sacrificed on the altar of political expediency.

The failings of these systems are not mere conjectures; they are realities that have been felt by every American. The economic crises that have gripped our nation are symptomatic of these deeper systemic issues. The Great Depression, the Great Recession, and the pandemic-induced economic downturns were not just natural fluctuations of the market; they were exacerbated, if not partly caused, by the shortcomings of our globalist pursuits and the limitations of our binary political structure.

Moreover, these systems have fostered a disconnect between the leaders and the led. The voices of the common people, the lifeblood of our nation, have been drowned out by the clamor of political elites and globalist interests. The time has come to cast off the yoke of these outdated systems, to forge a new path that is truly reflective of the will and the needs of the American people.

As we stand at the precipice of change, let us not be daunted by the magnitude of the task before us. The road to a new era of American greatness is paved with the lessons of our past. We must embrace a future that prioritizes national sovereignty, economic self-reliance, and a political system that is responsive to the needs of all Americans, not just the privileged few.

In this spirit, we must endeavor to create a new political movement, one that transcends the archaic divisions of Left and Right, and embodies the true spirit of American resilience and ingenuity. It is not just a call to action; it is a call to arms for all who believe in the promise of America, for all who are committed to the restoration of our nation's glory and the realization of its destiny.

In the face of our nation's trials and tribulations, a clarion call for transformation echoes across the land, heralding the dawn of a new political era. This is the call of American populism, a bold proposition for a future unshackled from the chains of outdated ideologies and systems that have long ceased to serve the common good. This movement is the embodiment of a national awakening, a resurgence of the true American spirit that has lain dormant for too long.

The foundation of American populism is built upon the unyielding bedrock of national pride and self-determination. It rejects the globalist agenda that has siphoned our strength and diluted our identity. Instead, it champions the cause of American sovereignty, advocating for policies that prioritize the welfare and prosperity of our own people above all else. It is a party that seeks to restore the balance of power, ensuring that the voices of the American people are heard and heeded in the halls of governance.

This movement stands as a bulwark against the divisive and often paralyzing nature of the two-party system. This new movement transcends traditional political boundaries, uniting Americans from all walks of life under a common banner of national renewal. It seeks to dismantle the partisan gridlock that has stifled progress and to replace it with a system that is responsive, dynamic, and truly representative of the American populace.

This new political movement has developed into One American Party. It is driven by a vision of unity and strength, where every citizen is empowered to contribute to the nation's prosperity. It envisions an America where opportunity is abundant, and success is determined not by one's connections or political affiliation, but by talent, hard work, and dedication to the common cause. It is a vision that revives the American Dream, making it accessible to all, irrespective of their background or station in life.

In addressing the needs of the American people, the One American Party proposes bold and innovative solutions to the pressing issues of our time. From revitalizing our economy and ensuring economic self-reliance, to reforming our education and healthcare systems, the party is committed to implementing policies that are grounded in practicality, efficiency, and, above all, the well-being of the American citizen.

The One American Party also recognizes the importance of cultural and spiritual rejuvenation. It seeks to foster a sense of national unity and identity, celebrating our rich heritage and the values that have made our country great. It advocates for a renaissance of American arts, literature, and traditions, cultivating a sense of pride and belonging among the people.

This is not merely a political proposal; it is a call to action for all who yearn for a return to true American greatness. It is an invitation to be part of a movement that will shape the destiny of our nation for generations to come. The One American Party stands as a beacon of hope, a testament to the indomitable will of the American people, and a promise of a future where our nation not only endures but thrives in the face of adversity.

In this era of unprecedented challenges and transformations, American populism emerges not merely as a political alternative but as a beacon of hope for a united and resolute nation. It carries with it a vision for American unity, a vision where the divisiveness that has long plagued our political and social landscapes is replaced by a renewed sense of national camaraderie and solidarity.

This vision transcends the superficial boundaries of class, race, and ideology that have been artificially imposed upon our people. It calls for a unification of the American spirit, a binding together of our diverse threads into a strong and vibrant tapestry. This unity is not born of uniformity; rather, it is a harmonious blend of our myriad voices, cultures, and experiences, coming together to form a more perfect union.

American populism understands that true unity cannot be mandated by decree; it must be nurtured in the hearts and minds of the people. It starts with a collective recommitment to the fundamental principles upon which our nation was founded—liberty, justice, and the pursuit of happiness. These principles are not relics of a bygone era; they are eternal beacons that guide our path forward.

To achieve this unity, the party proposes a cultural and educational renaissance, a reinvigoration of the American narrative. It envisions an education system that not only imparts skills and knowledge but also instills a deep appreciation for our history and values. Through this, future generations will inherit not just a land but a legacy—a legacy of freedom, courage, and indomitable will.

American populism is calling for a reclamation of the public discourse from the clutches of divisiveness and hostility. It encourages a dialogue that is grounded in respect and understanding, where differing viewpoints are not just tolerated but valued. This is the bedrock of a free society—a society where every voice is heard, and every person is seen.

In this vision for American unity, the party also emphasizes the importance of economic inclusivity. It advocates for policies that ensure every American has the opportunity to participate in and benefit from our nation's prosperity. This is not a pursuit of equality of outcome but an assurance of equality of opportunity—the chance for every citizen to achieve their full potential and contribute to the greater good.

The vision of populist patriotism is also one of resilience and adaptability in the face of change. It recognizes that the world is in a constant state of flux and that our unity must be dynamic, able to withstand and thrive amid the ebbs and flows of global shifts and internal transformations.

This vision for American unity is a call to every citizen who believes in the promise and potential of our great nation. It is an invitation to be part of a movement that is not defined by what divides us, but by what unites us. It is a journey toward realizing a more harmonious, prosperous, and dignified America—an America where every individual is part of a greater whole, and where that whole is greater than the sum of its parts.

The emergence of American populism heralds a new chapter, one where the enduring principles of populism and patriotism are not mere rhetoric, but the very bedrock of our political philosophy. This chapter is an ode to the unyielding spirit of the American people, a testament to their resolve to reclaim the essence of their nation from the grip of detached elites and partisan interests.

Populism, in its purest form, is the voice of the people resonating in the corridors of power. It is the assertion that the heart of America beats not in the isolated halls of governance but in the bustling streets, the rolling farmlands, the vibrant communities where the real America thrives. The One American Party embodies this populist ethos, championing the cause of the average citizen, advocating for their rights, their aspirations, their dreams. This is a movement that draws its strength not from the few, but from the many; not from the elite, but from the everyday American who yearns for a government that is responsive, accountable, and attuned to their needs.

Yet, populism without patriotism would be like a tree without roots. Patriotism, in the zeitgeist of this movement, is the profound love and commitment to our homeland. It is the recognition that our nation, with its rich history and cultural heritage, is worth cherishing, preserving, and defending. This patriotism is not blind allegiance, but a conscious and deliberate choice to uphold the ideals that have made America a beacon of hope and freedom across the world.

Americans finally seek to ignite a patriotic fervor, a collective pride in the accomplishments and virtues of our nation. It calls upon every American to embrace their heritage, to celebrate their identity as part of this great country. This patriotism is inclusive, embracing the diverse tapestry of experiences and backgrounds that constitute the American populace. It is a patriotism that recognizes that our differences do not weaken us, but rather, they are the source of our strength, the wellspring of our greatness.

In this vision, patriotism also means vigilance—vigilance against forces, both external and internal, that seek to undermine our sovereignty and erode our national values. The party advocates for policies that protect our borders, our industries, our culture, ensuring that America remains strong and self-reliant. It understands that true patriotism involves not just the celebration of our nation's glories but also the courage to confront its challenges and rectify its wrongs.

The union of populism and patriotism is a rallying cry for a new era of American governance. It is a call to return power to the people, to revitalize their love for their country, and to rekindle the flame of American exceptionalism. This is not a path devoid of obstacles, but it is a path that leads to a more representative, more vibrant, more united America.

As we embrace this melding of populism and patriotism, let us forge ahead with an unwavering conviction in our cause. Let this union be our guiding light, leading us toward a future where the American Dream is not a distant memory, but a living, breathing reality for every citizen. Together, under the banner of populist patriotism, we shall embark on this noble journey, charting a course toward a renewed era of American greatness.

As populist patriots stand poised to usher in a new epoch of American resurgence, we must acknowledge the formidable challenges that lie ahead. These obstacles, steeped in the vestiges of an old order resistant to change, demand not only our attention but our steadfast resolve to overcome. It is in this crucible of adversity that our collective strength and commitment to the ideals of our nation will be tested and ultimately proven.

The path to revitalizing our great nation is fraught with trials that test the very fibers of our resolve. The entrenched forces of the status quo, guardians of a bygone era, stand in opposition to the winds of change. The partisan gridlock that has long crippled our political process, the pervasive influence of special interests that seek to sway policy for their own gain, and the apathy and disillusionment that have taken root in the hearts of many citizens—these are but a few of the hurdles we face in our quest for national renewal.

Moreover, the specter of cynicism and doubt, cast by those who have lost faith in the promise of America, looms large. The challenge here is not only political but also moral and spiritual. It requires a rekindling of the American spirit, an awakening of the core values and beliefs that have been the bedrock of our nation's identity.

Yet, in the face of these daunting challenges, true Americans stand undeterred. Our movement draws upon the indomitable spirit of the American people, a spirit that has never faltered in the face of adversity. This spirit, imbued with a sense of purpose and destiny, is our most potent weapon against the trials that confront us.

To overcome the challenges that impede our progress, the populist patriotism movement is taking on a multifaceted approach. It calls for a reformation of our political process, breaking down the barriers of partisanship and opening the doors to a more inclusive and representative form of governance. This includes electoral reforms that give voice to the diverse array of opinions and perspectives that constitute the American polity.

Furthermore, the party recognizes the need for a cultural shift, a move away from divisiveness and toward a narrative of unity and common purpose. This involves a concerted effort to engage and empower citizens, to reinvigorate their sense of civic duty and pride in their country. It is a call for every American to be an active participant in the shaping of our nation's destiny.

In addition, we must emphasize the importance of economic revitalization as a cornerstone of overcoming our challenges. This entails the adoption of policies that promote growth, innovation, and sustainability, ensuring that America's economic engine is robust and capable of weathering the storms of global uncertainty.

The journey toward a renewed America is not one of ease or comfort. It is a journey that demands courage, conviction, and an unwavering belief in the greatness of our nation. The American Populist Movement, fortified by the will and determination of the American people, is ready to lead this journey.

Let us, therefore, march forward with a shared vision and a common goal. Let us face these challenges not as insurmountable obstacles, but as opportunities to demonstrate the true strength and character of our nation. Together, under the banner of populist patriotism, we will overcome these challenges, forging a future that is reflective of the highest ideals and aspirations of the American people. A future where our nation not only survives but thrives, standing as a beacon of hope, freedom, and prosperity for the world to behold.

As we stand at the threshold of a pivotal moment in our nation's history, the clarion call of this new American political movement resounds with a message of hope, renewal, and unyielding determination. This call is not just for a change in policy or leadership, but for a fundamental reawakening of the American spirit of self-determination. It is a call to reclaim our destiny, to steer our ship away from turbulent waters, guided by the stars of our enduring values and the compass of our collective will.

The journey we embark upon is not merely one of political transformation; it is a journey of national rebirth. It is a journey back to the principles that birthed our great nation—the principles of freedom, integrity, and the unalienable rights of every citizen. American populism stands as the vanguard of this journey, championing the cause of a people who have for too long been silenced, who have for too long watched the levers of power controlled by those who do not share their interests or their values.

Our vision of American self-determination is grounded in the belief that the strength of our nation lies in the hearts and minds of its people. It is they who should shape its future, not the detached elites, not the transnational interests that seek to dictate from afar. This is the essence of a republic—a government of the people, by the people, for the people.

Populist patriots envision a nation where every citizen is an architect of their own destiny, where the chains of dependency and disillusionment are broken, replaced by a renewed sense of purpose and possibility. This is a future where American innovation, resilience, and spirit are the driving forces behind our prosperity and global leadership.

As we forge this future, let us remember that the road to self-determination is not without its challenges. It requires a steadfast commitment to our ideals, a willingness to confront and overcome the obstacles that lie before us. It demands a collective effort, a unity of purpose that transcends political and social divides.

Let us also remember that self-determination is not an end, but a continual process. It is the constant striving to be better, to do better, for ourselves and for future generations. It is the relentless pursuit of a more perfect union, where each day we come closer to realizing the full potential of our great nation.

I call upon every patriot, every citizen who believes in the promise of America, to join in this noble endeavor. Together, we will write the next chapter in our nation's history—a chapter of renewal, of prosperity, of unparalleled greatness. It is time to seize our destiny, to take control of our future, and to reaffirm the eternal truth that in America, the power lies with the people.

Thus, let us move forward with unwavering resolve and unbreakable unity, ever mindful of the legacy we will leave for those who will follow in our footsteps. Let the spirit of American self-determination be our guide, our inspiration, and our enduring legacy. Together, we will reclaim our destiny and secure our place in history as a people of strength, honor, and indomitable resolve.

CHAPTER **8**

# AMERICAN PROSPERITY

———

In the heart of every true American lies a deep-seated conviction: the inseparable bond between economic and political freedom. This isn't just an idealistic chant but a fundamental truth, proven time and again through the annals of history. The nations that flourished, those bastions of innovation and prosperity, were not the ones shackled by overbearing governments, but rather those that breathed the air of economic liberty.

The leftist policies that have been paraded as saviors of the common man, on the other hand, have only served to betray the American people to the benefit of no one save members of the political class. In reality, these are nothing but chains in disguise, masquerading as welfare but serving to stifle the very essence of freedom. The narrative pushed by the Left is dangerously misleading—it promotes a vision of "equality" that ultimately leads to economic stagnation and political repression. When the government oversteps, dictating how you can earn, spend, and save, it's not just your wallet that's under siege—it's your fundamental liberties.

Let's be clear: economic freedom is the bedrock of self-actualization. It's about more than just making money. It's about the freedom to innovate, to take risks, and to reap the rewards of hard work. When individuals are empowered to pursue their economic interests, they're not just building wealth; they're carving out their destiny. This is the kind of empowerment that elevates a nation, fostering a society of individuals who are not only prosperous but also vested in the democratic process.

Look around. Wherever leftist ideologies have clamped down on economic freedom, political freedom has gasped for air. High taxes, overregulation, and bloated government bureaucracies don't just hamper business growth; they erode the very foundations of a free society. It's a simple equation: when the state controls the economy, it controls its citizens. And that's a scenario no true American would ever stand for.

It's crucial to recognize the threats posed by those advocating for increased government control under the guise of economic equality. The path to prosperity and freedom isn't through government handouts or restrictive economic policies. It's carved through the spirit of free enterprise, through the unyielding belief in the individual's right to economic self-determination.

The link between economic and political freedom is not just a theory; it's the cornerstone of our nation. It's a principle that must be defended fiercely against any ideology that seeks to weaken it. For in this battle lies the essence of our liberty, the future of our nation, and the hope of a better, freer world for generations to come.

In the relentless crusade against capitalism, the Left has been particularly adept at weaving a narrative riddled with misconceptions. They paint capitalism as the villain, the heartless monster feeding on the poor to fatten the rich. But this portrayal couldn't be further from the truth. It's a distorted picture, carefully crafted to undermine the very system that has lifted millions out of poverty and ignited the engines of innovation and progress.

Let's lay down the facts. Capitalism isn't about exploitation; it's about opportunity. It's not about greed; it's about growth. Across the globe, wherever capitalism has taken root, prosperity has followed. The story is clear and undeniable: free markets have been the greatest liberators of humanity from the clutches of poverty. The data speaks for itself—countries that embrace market principles boast higher standards of living, better healthcare, and greater opportunities for their citizens. This isn't a coincidence; it's the power of capitalism at work.

The Left's war on capitalism is fundamentally a war on wealth creation. By demonizing profits and vilifying entrepreneurs, they're attacking the very mechanisms that drive progress. Capitalism doesn't just create wealth for the few; it creates opportunities for the many. It incentivizes innovation, rewards hard work, and opens doors that would otherwise remain shut. The beauty of capitalism lies in its ability to empower individuals to turn their dreams into realities, to transform their visions into ventures.

The greatest exploitation we face today isn't from capitalism; it's from policies that strangle individual initiative under the guise of fairness. When the government steps in to "level the playing field," it often ends up doing the opposite. Overregulation, excessive taxation, and government interference don't level anything. They simply handicap the entrepreneurial spirit and dampen the dynamism that drives economic growth.

As defenders of truth and champions of the individual, we must stand firm against the tide of misinformation. We must uphold the virtues of capitalism, not as a perfect system, but as the best system we have for fostering innovation, prosperity, and freedom. The battle against these misconceptions is not just about defending an economic model; it's about preserving the essence of what makes our society thrive—the unyielding belief in the power of the individual to change the world for the better.

In the grand theater of modern politics, one of the most insidious acts is the government's overreach into our economic lives. It's a creeping vine, subtle yet suffocating, strangling the vitality out of our free market. This overreach isn't just an annoyance; it's a fundamental threat to our economic liberty. When the government dictates how businesses should operate, what prices they should set, and who they should hire, it's not "helping"—it's hindering, and it's doing so with a heavy hand.

This heavy hand extends beyond the realm of simple regulation to the very nature of money itself in our nation through the advent of the Federal Reserve, an institution shrouded in mystery and yet wielding immense power over our economy. Its decisions, often made behind closed doors, affect every American. The Fed's manipulation of interest rates and the money supply might seem like distant, abstract concepts, but they have real consequences: inflation, market bubbles, and economic cycles that leave hardworking Americans vulnerable. The question we must ask is: Should an unelected body have such control over our economic destiny?

The results of government meddling are as predictable as they are tragic. Take hyperinflation, a monster of the government's own making. It erodes savings, punishes the prudent, and hits the poorest the hardest. Then there's wealth disparity—a term the Left loves to throw around. But what they fail to acknowledge is that such disparity is often exacerbated by the government's actions. Excessive regulation and crony capitalism create an environment where only the big players can survive, squeezing out small businesses and widening the gap between the haves and have-nots.

Beware the government bearing gifts of "economic protection." These interventions, while cloaked in the language of support and fairness, are anything but. They stifle competition, discourage innovation, and lead to a stagnant economy where the average citizen struggles to advance. The irony is stark—in trying to "protect" us, the government often ends up doing the opposite.

The time has come to reclaim our economic freedom from the clutches of government overreach. We must advocate for policies that minimize government intervention, champion free enterprise, and trust individuals to make the best economic decisions for themselves and their families. It's a return to the fundamentals—a belief in the power of the free market and the resilience of the American spirit.

Government overreach and economic subjugation are not just policy issues; they're chains that bind the potential of every American. Breaking free from these chains requires vigilance, courage, and an unwavering commitment to the principles of economic freedom. The stakes couldn't be higher, for it is in this fight that the future prosperity and freedom of our nation lie.

At the heart of the populist patriots' vision lies a bold and uncompromising idea: a new social and economic contract, one that is steeped in the values of individual liberty and economic empowerment. This vision rejects the paternalistic approach of the government-knows-best mentality and instead places its trust in the hands of the people. It's a contract that understands that a nation's strength comes not from its bureaucrats but from its citizens, their dreams, and their entrepreneurial spirit.

This new vision calls for a radical shift in perspective—from dependency to empowerment, from government reliance to individual resilience. It's about rekindling the American spirit, that indomitable force that thrived on the frontier and sparked innovations that changed the world. The populist patriots' plan doesn't just offer economic policies; it offers a revival of the American ethos—the belief that each person holds within them the power to shape not only their destiny but that of the nation.

Fiscal responsibility is more than a policy; it's a principle. The reckless spending and ballooning deficits are not just numbers on a page; they are a looming threat to our economic sovereignty. The populist patriots' vision calls for a return to fiscal sanity—a world where budgets are balanced, spending is prudent, and debt is not a burden passed on to future generations. It's a vision that sees economic sustainability as the foundation of a free and prosperous society.

At the forefront of this vision is a commitment to peel back the layers of overregulation that suffocate businesses and stifle innovation. It's about creating an environment where entrepreneurs can thrive, where small businesses can grow without the fear of bureaucratic entanglement. Similarly, tax reduction will not be seen as a giveaway to the rich, but as a liberation of the economy, unshackling it from the heavy hand of government and allowing the free market to breathe and grow.

The populist patriots' vision heralds a return to American self-reliance. It's a call to reignite the pioneering spirit, to look within rather than abroad for solutions. This vision champions the idea of American exceptionalism—not as a boastful claim, but as a recognition of the unique blend of ingenuity, determination, and optimism that defines the American character. It's a vision that sees America not as a nation in decline, but as a land brimming with potential, ready for a new chapter of prosperity and greatness.

The populist patriots' economic vision is a clarion call for a return to the principles that made America great. It's a vision steeped in the belief in individual freedom, fiscal responsibility, and the power of the free market. This isn't just an economic plan; it's a road map to a future where every American has the opportunity to prosper, where the dreams of today forge the realities of tomorrow. It's a vision that looks forward with hope, grounded in the enduring principles that have always been the bedrock of America's greatness.

* * *

Manufacturing had always been the pulsating heart of traditional American economic principles in practice. Yet, in recent decades, this heart has been neglected, allowed to wither under policies that favored outsourcing and global dependency. The populist patriots' vision seeks to reverse this trend, to rekindle the flames of American industrial might. This revival isn't just about economics; it's about reclaiming a part of our national identity, an identity forged in the fires of industry and innovation.

The allure of cheaper labor and lower production costs overseas has led many to champion outsourcing. But let's be clear: the price of this short-term gain is a long-term loss. Outsourcing has not only led to the erosion of American manufacturing capabilities but has also made us vulnerable, dependent on foreign powers for essential goods. It's time to acknowledge the true cost of these policies—the loss of jobs, the decline of communities, and the weakening of our national security.

The vision for American manufacturing is one of resurgence and renaissance. It's a vision that sees factories humming once again in the heartland of America, where the "Made in the USA" label regains its old pride and prestige. This revival involves cutting the red tape that strangles domestic production, providing incentives for companies to bring manufacturing back to American shores, and investing in the technologies and skills that will propel us into the future.

American manufacturing should not just be about quantity; it should be a beacon of quality and innovation. The world knows that when America makes something, it's made to last, made with skill, and made with ingenuity. Reviving manufacturing is about harnessing the American spirit of innovation—a spirit that took us to the moon and back, that built skyscrapers and Silicon Valley. It's about creating products that don't just serve needs but inspire awe.

Let's not forget the social fabric of our nation, woven through the mills and factories that once dotted the American landscape. Reviving manufacturing is about more than economics; it's about rebuilding communities. It's about providing dignified, fulfilling work that supports families and nurtures towns. This vision of manufacturing is about restoring the pride of the American worker, the pride that comes from building something with one's own hands, something that contributes not just to the economy but to the nation's spirit.

The restoration of American manufacturing is a central pillar of the populist patriots' economic vision. It's about bringing back jobs, yes, but it's also about reviving the American spirit of enterprise and self-reliance. It's a call to arms, to rebuild the industrial might that once made America the envy of the world. This is more than an economic policy; it's a rallying cry for a nation ready to roll up its sleeves and get back to work, building a future as durable and enduring as the products it aims to create.

When it comes to the economic might of a people, their nation's currency holds a place of central importance. The populist patriots envision a currency that stands as a testament to American resilience and stability. This vision calls for a currency backed by tangible assets like gold or grounded in the cutting-edge technology of blockchain. Such a currency wouldn't just be a medium of exchange; it would be a symbol of American economic sovereignty, a bulwark against the whims of international markets and the pitfalls of fiat currency devaluation.

The Federal Reserve, an institution shrouded in mystery and complexity, wields enormous influence over our economy. Yet, its operations remain largely unchecked and opaque. The call to audit the Federal Reserve is not a call for conspiracy; it's a call for accountability and transparency. Americans deserve to know how decisions that affect their daily lives are made, how their currency is managed, and how their economic destiny is shaped. An audited Federal Reserve is a step toward demystifying this power and placing it under the rightful scrutiny of the people.

In an era where digital transactions are becoming the norm, protecting financial privacy becomes paramount. The populist patriots' vision upholds the principle that an individual's financial dealings are their own business. This vision recognizes the looming threats in an increasingly interconnected world, where data is as valuable as currency. Safeguarding financial privacy isn't just about preventing identity theft or fraud; it's about preserving the fundamental liberty of individuals to control their economic life without undue surveillance or intrusion.

The push for a strong currency backed by gold or blockchain is more than an economic policy; it's a statement of confidence in the American economy. A strong currency reflects a strong nation, one that is not subject to the volatility of global financial winds. It's a currency that instills confidence in investors, stability in markets, and pride in the citizens. This vision seeks a currency that is not just a tool of trade but a reflection of the enduring strength and resilience of the American economy.

The populist patriots' financial vision is a bold reimagining of America's financial landscape. It's a vision that looks to the future, embracing innovation and technology while staying grounded in the timeless principles of transparency, accountability, and privacy. This vision proposes a financial system that is robust yet flexible, powerful yet accountable, and innovative yet secure.

The currency and financial policies outlined by the populist patriots are pivotal in shaping a future where America's economic strength is unassailable. It's a future where the American dollar is as respected and reliable as the nation it represents. This vision is not just about maintaining economic stability; it's about asserting America's economic leadership in a rapidly evolving global landscape. It's a vision that ensures America's financial system remains the cornerstone of its economic might and a beacon of trust and stability in an uncertain world.

As the world is increasingly drawn toward globalization, we must stand firm on the principle of ethical and balanced trade. This vision challenges the status quo of international trade practices that have often left American interests and workers in the lurch. The call here is for trade policies that are fair, reciprocal, and, most importantly, beneficial to the American economy and its people. This approach doesn't shun global trade but insists that it be conducted on terms that respect American labor, protect our industries, and preserve our economic sovereignty.

A cornerstone of this new economic vision is the innovative approach to revenue generation through tariffs. In an era where the typical response to fiscal shortfalls has been to hike up taxes, the populist patriots propose a shift toward tariff-based revenue. This isn't a return to mercantilism, but a strategic use of tariffs to protect American industries and generate revenue without burdening American taxpayers. It's a policy that recognizes the value of domestic production and the importance of safeguarding it from unfair foreign competition.

In the realm of taxation, let's bring forth a bold proposal to overhaul the capital gains tax. This vision sees a shift toward an automated capital gains tax on stock market trades—a move that promises to streamline tax collection and ensure fairness. This isn't about penalizing success; it's about ensuring that the financial sector contributes its fair share to the nation's economy. By implementing this automated system, the aim is to create a more efficient, transparent, and equitable tax process.

Central to this vision is a staunch opposition to the overbearing tax burden that stifles American families and businesses. The call is for a significant reduction in taxes, freeing individuals and enterprises from the heavy hand of excessive government levies. This approach is grounded in the belief that lower taxes lead to economic growth, empowering individuals and businesses to invest, innovate, and expand.

The reimagining of tax policy is not just about reducing the tax burden; it's about using tax policy as a tool for empowerment and economic revitalization. It's a vision that aligns tax policy with the broader goals of economic freedom, self-reliance, and prosperity. By reforming trade and tax policies, the aim is to unleash the full potential of the American economy, fostering an environment where businesses can thrive, jobs are plentiful, and prosperity is shared.

The trade and tax policies envisioned by American populism represent a radical departure from the status quo. They are policies that seek to position America favorably in the global economy while ensuring the prosperity and well-being of its citizens. This vision is a clarion call for policies that protect American interests, promote fairness, and foster an economic environment where every American can thrive. It's a vision that looks beyond mere economic metrics, seeing trade and tax policies as integral components of a larger narrative of American strength, sovereignty, and success.

It's long been a sacred component of the American Dream to own a home. Yet, for too many Americans, this dream is slipping away, buried under the weight of policies that inflate prices and limit availability. Americans recognize this crisis not just as an economic issue, but as a fundamental challenge to the American ethos. The vision presented is bold and unyielding: to reshape housing policies in a way that reignites the possibility of homeownership for every American, from the bustling cities to the quiet rural towns.

The policies of the Left, though often wrapped in the rhetoric of compassion and support, have failed to deliver on their promises. Excessive regulation, misguided zoning laws, and government overreach have not only stifled the construction of new homes but have also driven up costs, making homeownership an elusive dream for many. These policies, while claiming to protect, have instead become barriers, locking out countless Americans from a fundamental aspect of their pursuit of happiness, a pursuit mired with the burden of ever-increasing taxation.

An elimination of personal income and property taxes in relation to homeownership is in order. This approach challenges the traditional revenue models, advocating instead for a system that encourages ownership and investment in property. The elimination of these taxes would not only relieve financial pressure on homeowners but also stimulate the housing market, making the dream of owning a home a tangible reality for more Americans.

To compensate for the revenue lost through these tax cuts, the vision proposes a novel approach: relying on tariff-based revenue and an automated capital gains tax on stock market trades. This strategy seeks to shift the tax burden away from everyday Americans, placing it instead on areas of the economy that can sustain it without direct impact on the individual citizen. It's a bold reimagining of fiscal policy, one that aligns with the principles of fairness and economic empowerment.

A populist vision for housing is deeply intertwined with the broader narrative of the American Dream. It's a vision that sees a nation where homeownership is accessible, where communities can flourish without the shadow of unaffordable housing. This policy is about more than bricks and mortar; it's about restoring the promise of America, a promise where hard work and determination are rewarded with a piece of the American pie.

It's time for a revolutionary approach to housing and taxation that is deeply rooted in the American tradition of self-reliance and individual freedom. These policies are an approach that seeks to dismantle the barriers erected by misguided policies and replace them with a framework that empowers citizens, revitalizes communities, and rekindles the flame of the American Dream. This vision for housing is not just a set of policies; it's a blueprint for a future where homeownership is once again a central pillar of American life, accessible to all who dare to dream. Yet, the details of housing and taxation are irrelevant without addressing the overarching philosophical and political conflict Americans have been the victim of for decades.

In the grand scheme of economic strategies, a pivotal battle rages between national and globalist economic models. True Americans stand unwaveringly on the side of national economics, advocating for policies that put America first. This isn't about isolationism; it's about prioritizing American interests, ensuring that our economic policies serve the American people first and foremost. In contrast, globalist approaches often dilute national sovereignty, subjecting domestic economies to the whims of international bodies and foreign interests. The choice is clear: a national economy that serves its people, or a globalist one that serves multinational conglomerates.

At the core of economic strength lies control over fiscal policy and the money supply. The populist patriots advocate for policies that ensure fiscal discipline, reduce national debt, and keep the control of money within national borders. This vision opposes reckless government spending and the unchecked printing of money, actions that devalue currency and erode economic stability. By asserting control over fiscal policy and the money supply, the goal is to build an economy that is robust, self-sustaining, and immune to external economic shocks.

Central to a new populist American economic philosophy is the role of government. Instead of being a provider, meddling in every aspect of the economy, the government should be a protector—safeguarding free-market principles, ensuring fair play, and providing the necessary infrastructure for economic growth. This vision advocates for a government that sets the stage for economic success but then steps back, allowing the ingenuity and drive of the American people to take center stage.

These broader economic themes paint a picture of an America that is economically strong, sovereign, and just. This vision challenges the status quo, advocating for a reimagining of economic policies and priorities. It's a vision that sees America not just as an economic powerhouse but as a nation where prosperity is shared, where economic policy is aligned with the values of freedom, self-reliance, and fairness. In this vision lies the path to an America that is not only prosperous but also proud, resilient, and true to the ideals upon which it was founded.

## CHAPTER 9

# RISE OF AMERICAN POPULISM

In the current landscape of the United States, the economic and political conditions are marked by a distinct and palpable tension. The nation, once a beacon of unbridled opportunity and prosperity, now grapples with challenges that seem to undermine the very foundations of its celebrated ideals.

The American economy, often hailed as the strongest and most dynamic in the world, is showing signs of strain. Despite reports of growth and stock market successes, the reality for the average American paints a different picture. The cost of living has soared, yet wages remain stubbornly stagnant for the working and middle classes. This disparity is not just a number on a spreadsheet; it's a daily struggle for millions trying to make ends meet.

Inflation, a word that echoes ominously in the corridors of power, has ceased to be a mere economic term. It has become a tangible, bitter reality for families across the nation. The prices of essentials, from groceries to healthcare, have risen dramatically, eating away at the purchasing power of the average citizen. This inflation is not an act of God; it's a consequence of policy decisions, a by-product of an economic system that seems increasingly rigged against the everyday American.

Politically, the country is more divided than ever. The chasm between the Left and Right has widened, with both sides seemingly entrenched in their ideological fortresses. This polarization is more than just a disagreement over policy; it's a fundamental clash over the vision for America's future.

On one side, there's a growing push for policies that prioritize global interests, often at the expense of national ones. The sovereignty of the United States, a principle once held sacrosanct, is now frequently called into question. The focus seems to have shifted from "America First" to a nebulous form of internationalism that dilutes the country's unique identity and values.

On the other side, there's a resurgence of a more traditional, nationalistic perspective. This viewpoint emphasizes the importance of American sovereignty, the need to prioritize domestic interests, and a skepticism of overreaching global institutions. The debate is not just political; it's a cultural battle for the heart and soul of America.

The economic struggles and political divisions have a profound impact on the nation's psyche. The American Dream, once attainable for anyone willing to work hard, now seems like a distant memory for many. The fabric of society, woven from the threads of unity, hard work, and shared prosperity, is fraying.

In this climate of uncertainty and change, the call for a new approach is growing louder. A yearning for policies that resonate with the experiences and challenges of the average American is emerging. People are seeking leadership that understands and addresses the realities of those outside the power corridors of Washington.

As we navigate these complex and turbulent times, the need for a clear, pragmatic, and compassionate vision for America has never been greater. The nation stands at a crossroads, where the decisions made today will shape the future for generations to come. It is a moment that calls for wisdom, courage, and an unwavering commitment to the principles that have long defined the greatness of America.

In the contemporary American saga, the chapter on economic struggles is both profound and distressing. The nation, which has long prided itself on being a land of opportunity, is witnessing a growing disconnect between the hallowed promises of the American Dream and the stark realities faced by its citizens.

The narrative often spun by those in positions of power speaks of economic recovery and resilience. Yet, for the average American, this story feels like a distant myth. The working class, the backbone of this great nation, confronts a relentless onslaught of financial burdens. Their wages, stagnant for decades, barely keep pace with the escalating cost of living. This isn't just an economic issue; it's a crisis of dignity and fairness.

The American worker, once assured of a stable and prosperous future through hard work and dedication, now faces uncertainty and insecurity. Jobs, many of which have been shipped overseas in the name of globalization, are increasingly scarce and undervalued. The hard truth is that the economic system, as it stands, seems to favor the elite, leaving the average worker to grapple with the fallout of decisions made in corporate boardrooms and political backrooms.

Inflation, a stealthy and insidious force, has further eroded the financial stability of many Americans. This is not just an economic challenge; it's a moral one. The value of hard-earned savings diminishes as prices soar, effectively serving as a covert form of taxation on the working class. This phenomenon isn't merely a result of market forces; it is, in many ways, a consequence of deliberate policy choices, including the practices of fractional reserve banking and the relentless printing of money.

These practices, often shrouded in complex economic jargon, have a very real and detrimental impact on the average person. The purchasing power of the dollar dwindles, savings erode, and the dream of financial security becomes ever more elusive. This is a betrayal of the fundamental principles of fairness and economic justice that America purports to uphold.

The economic system, as it currently operates, places an undue burden on the working class. The promise of America was that hard work would be rewarded with a fair share in its prosperity. However, this promise seems to be fading into the background, replaced by a system that benefits the few at the expense of the many.

The working class, already grappling with the challenges of a changing economy, is further burdened by a tax system that seems to favor the wealthy and powerful. The disparities in wealth and income are not just numbers on a chart; they represent a growing divide in the lived experiences of Americans. This divide challenges the very notion of fairness and equality that is supposed to be at the heart of the American ethos.

As we consider the economic struggles in the United States, it becomes increasingly clear that the status quo is unsustainable. The need for a system that truly represents and serves the interests of the average American has never been more urgent. The nation's economic policies must be reevaluated and reformed to ensure that the promise of America is a reality for all its citizens, not just a privileged few.

In the unfolding narrative of the United States, a worrying theme has emerged—the gradual erosion of its political and economic sovereignty. This decline is not just a matter of national pride; it's a profound shift that threatens the very essence of what it means to be American.

The term *globalism* is often heralded as a path to worldwide cooperation and progress. However, for many Americans, globalism has come to represent a loss of control over their own destiny. The policies and agreements made in the name of global cooperation have, in many cases, sidelined the interests of the American people in favor of international agendas.

Trade agreements, for instance, have been touted as a means to boost the global economy. Yet, the reality for the American worker has been starkly different. Factories have closed, jobs have vanished, and entire communities have been left desolate in the wake of these so-called "progressive" policies. The pursuit of global economic integration has often come at a high cost—the sacrifice of American jobs and industries.

The notion of American sovereignty extends beyond economics; it's a matter of having a say in the future direction of the nation. As global institutions and alliances grow in influence, the ability of the United States to chart its own course seems increasingly constrained. Decisions that significantly impact American lives are frequently made in international forums, where the voice and interests of the American people are just one of many, often overshadowed by global consensus.

This shift is not just a theoretical concern; it's a practical one. The policies and regulations crafted in distant offices and international conferences directly affect the lives of everyday Americans. From environmental regulations to trade policies, the hand of international influence is increasingly felt, often without the direct consent of the American populace.

The question that arises from this scenario is clear: Should the future of America be decided by global consensus or by the American people? For many, the answer is unequivocal—the destiny of America should be in the hands of Americans. There's a growing sentiment that the time has come to reassert the nation's sovereignty, to reclaim the right to decide its own economic and political future.

The call for a reassertion of sovereignty is not a call for isolationism; it is a demand for fair play and self-determination. It's about ensuring that the decisions impacting American lives are made with the interests of the American people at the forefront. This is not just a matter of policy; it's a matter of principle.

As the United States grapples with these challenges, the need for a clear and assertive stance on sovereignty becomes increasingly evident. The future of the nation depends not just on its economic might or military power, but on its ability to control its own destiny in an ever-changing global landscape. The loss of sovereignty is not just a loss for America; it's a loss for the ideals of self-governance and independence that have long defined the American spirit.

In the current American socio-political tapestry, a new thread has emerged, vibrant yet controversial—the rise of leftism and woke ideologies. These ideologies, while advocating for progressive changes, have sparked a debate about their impact on the cultural and moral fabric of the nation.

Leftism and woke ideologies have made their mark on American culture, permeating various aspects of social and political life. They advocate for a radical reshaping of societal norms and values, often challenging traditional concepts of identity, nationhood, and personal responsibility. While their proponents argue for inclusivity and social justice, critics see these ideologies as a departure from the core principles that have long underpinned American society.

One of the key criticisms is the perceived overemphasis on identity politics. This focus, while aimed at promoting diversity and addressing historical injustices, is often seen as creating divisions rather than unity. It emphasizes differences over commonalities, leading to a fragmentation of the national identity. The narrative, which often categorizes people into groups based on race, gender, and other characteristics, can overlook the individual's unique experiences and contributions, reducing complex human beings to mere representatives of their group identities.

Critics argue that the rise of these ideologies has led to a moral and cultural shift that undermines traditional values. This shift includes a move away from concepts like meritocracy, personal responsibility, and the importance of family structure. The emphasis on collective guilt and victimhood narratives, according to detractors, does not empower individuals but rather entraps them in a perpetual cycle of blame and dependency.

Another significant concern is the impact on freedom of speech and thought. The pursuit of a singularly "correct" way of thinking, often enforced through social pressure and public shaming, is viewed as an encroachment on the fundamental freedoms that America stands for. This "cancel culture" phenomenon, where individuals or entities are ostracized for views that deviate from the accepted narrative, is seen as a threat to open discourse and the marketplace of ideas.

While the intentions behind leftist and woke ideologies may, as unlikely as it is, stem from a desire to create a more equitable society, the approach and methods have become a point of contention. There is a growing call for a more balanced approach that recognizes the need for social progress while respecting traditional American values and principles.

The challenge lies in fostering a society that is inclusive and just, yet firmly rooted in the principles of individual liberty, free speech, and the pursuit of the American Dream. This balance is crucial for maintaining social cohesion and ensuring that the United States remains a nation where diverse ideas and perspectives can coexist and flourish.

The critique of leftism and woke ideologies is not merely a political disagreement; it is a reflection of a deeper struggle over the soul of American culture. It's a debate about how to navigate the complexities of a modern, diverse society while holding on to the values that have long defined the American ethos.

Amid the economic landscape of the United States, a critical question looms large: Who truly benefits from the current system? This question isn't just about numbers and statistics; it's about fairness, equity, and the American principle of opportunity for all.

At the heart of the American economic system, there exists a glaring disparity. While the average American grapples with stagnant wages and escalating living costs, a small segment of society reaps disproportionate benefits. This elite, a blend of corporate magnates and high-ranking political figures, often operate within a sphere where power and wealth are mutually reinforcing.

The intertwining of corporate and political interests has led to policies that often favor the wealthy. Tax structures, regulatory frameworks, and government contracts are manipulated in ways that disproportionately benefit those at the top. This is not the free-market capitalism that America champions; it's a distorted system where success is less about innovation and hard work and more about access and influence.

The flip side of this equation is the American working class, bearing the brunt of a system skewed in favor of the powerful. These are the people who build, maintain, and drive the nation forward with their labor and perseverance. Yet, they find themselves in an economic structure that offers them a shrinking slice of the pie.

The realities are stark: wage stagnation, job insecurity, and a rising cost of living. The working class watches as their ability to achieve the American Dream slips further away, not due to a lack of effort or ambition, but because the deck seems stacked against them. The promise of upward mobility, once a cornerstone of American ethos, now feels more elusive than ever.

The political class, in tandem with economic elites, play a pivotal role in perpetuating these disparities. Through a combination of policymaking and influence, they have shaped an economic environment that serves their interests. This is a departure from the ideal of government as a representative of the people, working toward the collective good.

The result is a growing sense of disillusionment and frustration among the masses. The perception that the system is rigged, that the American Dream is becoming a privilege of the few rather than a promise for all, is a source of deep societal unrest.

The economic beneficiaries of the current system are a testament to a larger issue—the need for a recalibration of the American economic model. This recalibration is not about penalizing success but ensuring that the system is in line with the principles upon which the nation was built.

Addressing these inequities is not just a matter of economic policy; it's a matter of restoring faith in the American Dream. It's about creating a system where hard work and merit are rewarded, where the playing field is level, and where the promise of America is accessible to every citizen. The path forward requires a recommitment to the principles of fairness, opportunity, and the shared prosperity that has long been the hallmark of the American experience.

In the evolving tapestry of American society, a striking contrast has emerged between traditional American work ethics and contemporary leftist perspectives. This contrast is not just a matter of differing opinions; it represents a fundamental divergence in views on work, success, and the role of the individual in society.

The traditional American work ethic is rooted in principles of individualism, hard work, and personal responsibility. It's a legacy of a culture that values self-reliance, the pursuit of excellence, and the belief that hard work is the key to success. This ethos has been a driving force behind America's economic might and innovative spirit.

Under this paradigm, success is seen as achievable for anyone willing to put in the effort. The narrative is one of empowerment—the idea that through determination and perseverance, every individual has the opportunity to rise and achieve their dreams. This work ethic has been a cornerstone of American identity, encapsulating the spirit of optimism and the pursuit of the American Dream.

In stark contrast, contemporary leftist perspectives offer a different view on work and success. These views often emphasize structural challenges and societal inequities as primary barriers to success. There is a focus on collective responsibility and the role of the state in ensuring equitable outcomes for all individuals.

This perspective argues that factors like socio-economic background, race, and gender play a significant role in determining one's opportunities and success. As a result, there is a call for greater government intervention to level the playing field. While the intent is to promote fairness and social justice, critics argue that this approach can undermine the values of hard work and personal responsibility.

The contrast between these two perspectives has profound implications for societal and economic structures. The traditional work ethic champions a free-market economy where individuals are the primary drivers of their destiny. In contrast, the leftist view leans toward a more regulated economy where the government plays a significant role in redistributing resources and opportunities.

This divergence leads to debates on a range of issues, from welfare policies to business regulations. The traditional view warns of the dangers of an over reliant society, where excessive government intervention can stifle initiative and innovation. On the other hand, the leftist perspective raises concerns about an unequal society, where systemic barriers prevent many from realizing their potential.

The challenge for America lies in finding a middle ground that respects the traditional values of hard work and personal responsibility while acknowledging and addressing the legitimate concerns about social and economic inequalities. This balance is crucial for maintaining a society that is both dynamic and just.

The goal should be to create an environment where the traditional American work ethic can thrive in harmony with a fair system. It's about fostering a society where hard work is rewarded, opportunities are accessible, and every individual has the chance to write their own story of success. This balanced approach is key to preserving the essence of the American Dream—a dream that is inclusive, empowering, and reflective of the nation's diverse and evolving character.

In the contemporary American political spectrum, a resurgence of populist ideologies has taken center stage, reflecting a growing dissatisfaction with the status quo. This resurgence is not merely a political phenomenon; it's a cultural movement, rooted in the profound sentiments of a significant portion of the American populace.

Populist ideologies are primarily centered around the idea of returning power to the common people. This perspective is born out of a sense of disenchantment with the political and economic elites, who are perceived to be out of touch with the everyday struggles and values of the average citizen.

One of the fundamental tenets of populism is the emphasis on national sovereignty and the interests of the nation-state. Populists advocate for policies that prioritize the nation's needs, viewing globalism and internationalism with skepticism. This focus on national interests encompasses issues like immigration, trade, and foreign policy, where the emphasis is on protecting and advancing the welfare of the home country.

Another critical aspect of populist ideologies is the championing of economic fairness. The American populist argument is that the current economic system is rigged in favor of the elite, and populists advocate for policies that ensure a more equitable distribution of wealth and opportunities. This includes support for protecting jobs, revitalizing domestic industries, and challenging the power of large corporations and financial institutions.

Populists call for a return to what they see as core American values—a society that values hard work, personal responsibility, and a sense of community. They envision an America where the government is responsive to the needs of its citizens, rather than serving the interests of a disconnected elite.

This call for a return to populist values also includes a strong emphasis on cultural integrity. Populists often voice concerns about the dilution of national identity and the impact of liberal social policies on traditional values and norms. There is a sense of urgency to preserve the cultural heritage and societal framework that they believe has defined the American experience.

The rise of populist ideologies reflects a broader sense of unrest and discontent in modern America. This unrest stems from issues like economic inequality, perceived erosion of national sovereignty, and disillusionment with the political establishment. Populism, in this context, is seen as a response to these challenges, offering a vision of America that seeks to rectify these perceived imbalances.

The populist movement calls for a reevaluation of the relationship between the citizen and the state, advocating for a system that is more reflective of and responsive to the needs of the average American. It's a movement that seeks to redefine the political narrative, focusing on the empowerment of those who feel left behind by the current economic and political order.

In essence, the outline of populist ideologies represents a longing for a return to a more straightforward, transparent, and fair America. It's a call for a nation where the government is a true reflection of the people's will, where economic policies are fair and just, and where national interests are prioritized. Whether these ideologies will reshape the American political landscape remains to be seen, but their emergence is a clear sign of the changing dynamics in the nation's socio-political fabric.

In the evolving narrative of the United States, a fundamental truth has come to the forefront: the inextricable link between economic prosperity and political freedom. This connection is not merely a theoretical concept; it is the cornerstone of the American ethos and a key to understanding the nation's past successes and future potential.

Political freedom in America has always been more than just a right; it's a defining characteristic of the nation's identity. It's the freedom to speak, to think, to innovate, and to challenge the status quo. This freedom is the bedrock upon which the country was built, attracting generations of individuals seeking the liberty to pursue their dreams.

However, this political freedom is not just an end in itself; it's also a means to achieve economic prosperity. A society where individuals are free to express their ideas, to start businesses, and to engage in commerce without undue interference, is a society that cultivates innovation and economic growth. It's in this environment of freedom that creativity flourishes and new opportunities are born.

The American economy has historically thrived when political freedoms were upheld and respected. The country's history is replete with stories of individuals who, given the freedom to pursue their ambitions, have created economic value not only for themselves but for the nation as a whole. From small business owners to tech innovators, the American Dream has been fueled by the freedom to strive and succeed.

Conversely, when political freedoms are curtailed, economic prosperity often suffers. Overregulation, excessive government control, and limitations on free speech and expression can stifle innovation and discourage investment. The vitality of the American economy is directly tied to the extent to which its citizens are free to pursue economic activities.

In this context, there's a growing advocacy for less government intervention in both the economic and personal lives of citizens. The argument is that when the government oversteps its bounds, it not only infringes on individual freedoms but also hampers economic growth. The call is for a return to a more laissez-faire approach, where the market is allowed to function with minimal government interference.

This perspective champions the idea that the best way to ensure economic prosperity is to ensure political freedom. It's a belief in the power of the individual, in the entrepreneurial spirit, and in the market's ability to self-regulate and produce the best outcomes for the greatest number of people.

The relationship between economic prosperity and political freedom is a symbiotic one. Each feeds into and reinforces the other. A politically free society creates an environment conducive to economic growth, and a prosperous economy strengthens and supports a free society.

As America looks to the future, recognizing and nurturing this relationship will be crucial. The challenge lies in balancing the role of government in ensuring fairness and stability while preserving the freedoms that ignite economic dynamism. It's a delicate equilibrium, but one that is essential for the continued prosperity and freedom of the American people.

The American political landscape is a dynamic and ever-evolving arena, marked by the influential roles of both the Right and the Left. As the nation sails through turbulent times, understanding the interplay and future trajectories of these two political spectrums is crucial for anticipating the direction in which America is headed.

On the Right, the political philosophy is anchored in principles of conservatism, advocating for limited government intervention, individual liberties, and traditional values. This perspective emphasizes the importance of a free-market economy, national sovereignty, and a strong defense. The Right has been a champion of what many see as the core tenets of the American identity—self-reliance, personal responsibility, and a commitment to the nation's founding principles.

The Left, conversely, embodies a more progressive approach. It advocates for broader government intervention in the economy and social issues, emphasizing the need for social justice, equity, and environmental sustainability. The Left seeks to address systemic inequalities and champions policies that promote inclusivity, diversity, and a more global perspective in addressing international challenges.

Both sides bring vital perspectives to the national discourse, representing the diverse views and values of the American populace. However, the current political climate has seen an intensification of polarization, with both sides often entrenched in their positions, leading to a gridlock that hinders effective governance.

The future of American politics hinges on the ability of both sides to navigate this polarization. There is a growing need for dialogue and compromise, for finding common ground amid differing viewpoints. The challenges facing the nation—economic disparities, social injustices, environmental concerns, and international dynamics—require collaborative solutions that transcend political divisions.

The Right and the Left must recognize that the strength of America lies in its diversity of thought and the ability to unite under shared national ideals. The future calls for a political landscape where differences are not just tolerated but valued as a means to forge comprehensive and effective policies.

The impacts of political polarization extend beyond legislative stalemates; they permeate the very fabric of society, affecting how Americans interact with one another and view the role of government in their lives. A continued state of division risks eroding the sense of national unity and the ability to collectively address the critical issues of the day.

In this context, the role of the media, educational institutions, and civic organizations becomes increasingly important. These entities can either exacerbate divisions or act as bridges, fostering a culture of understanding, respect, and constructive debate.

As the United States moves forward, the role and future of the Right and Left in American politics will be pivotal in shaping the nation's trajectory. The task ahead is not to eliminate differences, but to leverage them in building a more prosperous, just, and unified country.

The hope for America lies in transcending the divide, in harnessing the best of both conservative and progressive ideals to forge a future that honors the nation's heritage while boldly addressing the challenges of a new era. It's a future where political discourse is marked not by animosity but by a shared commitment to the common good, a future where the American experiment continues to thrive and inspire.

The American Populist Movement, emerging as a forceful voice in the nation's political discourse, is built upon a set of foundational beliefs and principles. This movement, rooted in the concerns and aspirations of a significant segment of the American populace, seeks to redefine the relationship between the people and their government.

At its core, the populist movement is grounded in the belief that the ordinary citizen should be at the forefront of political decision-making. It asserts that the true power of a nation lies not in its elites or institutions, but in the hands of its people. This belief is a reclamation of the democratic ethos upon which America was founded—a government of the people, by the people, for the people.

The movement also emphasizes the importance of national sovereignty and the preservation of American values and interests. It views globalism with caution, advocating for policies that prioritize the nation's well-being over international commitments. This perspective champions a robust national identity, one that respects the country's heritage and traditions while navigating the complexities of the modern world.

The American Populist Movement is more than a set of policies; it's a call for a new direction in American politics. It's a response to feelings of disenfranchisement and neglect by the political establishment. This movement seeks to bring the concerns of the average American to the forefront, advocating for a political and economic system that is more inclusive, representative, and just.

The foundations and principles of the American Populist Movement represent a significant shift in the political landscape. It's a movement driven by the desire for a government that truly reflects the will and needs of its people. As this movement gains momentum, it has the potential to reshape the policies and priorities of the nation, steering

America toward a future that aligns with the aspirations and values of its populace.

In the current epoch of American politics and society, there is a resonating call for a new faith and direction. This call is not just a political rallying cry; it is a profound expression of a collective yearning for a reinvigoration of the principles and values that have long defined the American spirit.

This call for a new direction is a response to the growing sense of disillusionment with the existing political and economic systems. Many Americans feel that their voices are unheard, their concerns unaddressed, and their values unrepresented. There's a palpable desire for a political renaissance, one that brings back the focus on the ordinary citizen, their rights, and their welfare.

The new direction sought is one that diverges from the path of divisive politics, bureaucratic overreach, and disconnection from the grassroots. It's a call for a political framework that is transparent and aligned with the true aspirations of the American people. This includes a recommitment to the principles of liberty, justice, and the pursuit of happiness.

Central to this call is an encouragement to return to foundational American values. These values—individual freedom, hard work, community spirit, and national unity—have been the bedrock of the nation's identity. There's a sense that these values need to be rekindled and reaffirmed in the face of changing societal norms and challenges.

This return to foundational values is not about regressing to the past; it's about drawing on the enduring principles that have guided America through times of turmoil and triumph. It's about restoring a sense of pride and faith in what it means to be American, in the unique experiment in democracy and freedom that the United States represents.

The call for a new direction also involves a critical evaluation and often a rejection of certain globalist and leftist influences that are perceived to be at odds with American values and interests. There's a growing sentiment that these influences undermine national sovereignty, economic independence, and cultural integrity.

The focus is on reasserting America's autonomy in making its own decisions, both economically and politically, without undue external influence. This includes revisiting trade agreements, immigration policies, and international commitments to ensure that they serve the national interest.

This moment in America's history is seen as a pivotal one, a time for reflection and resurgence. It's a period where the nation reevaluates its direction, priorities, and values. The call for a new faith and direction is about envisioning a future that honors the legacy of the past while boldly addressing the challenges of the present and future.

It's a call for an America that is confident, proud, and united: an America that holds true to its founding ideals while forging a path that ensures prosperity, justice, and liberty for all its citizens. This is more than just a political movement; it's a cultural awakening, a reclamation of the American Dream in its most authentic and aspirational form.

CHAPTER 10

# LEFTISM

In the hallowed halls of America's esteemed universities, a quiet but seismic shift began to unfurl decades ago. It was here, amid the ivy-covered buildings and academic discourse, that the seeds of a profound ideological transformation were planted. This transformation was not merely academic; it was the genesis of a new era in American political and social thought. The protagonist of this evil narrative? Marxism.

The inception of Marxism into the fabric of American higher education was neither sudden nor blatant. It crept in, subtly at first, in the form of intellectual discourse and theoretical exploration. Professors and academics, many of whom were enamored by the romantic allure of Marxist theory, began to integrate these concepts into their teachings. The appeal was understandable—Marxism, with its critique of capitalistic exploitation and promise of a classless society, seemed like a panacea to the ills of the modern world. But was it?

As this ideology took root in academic settings, it began to influence not just the minds of students, but the very nature of political and economic discussions within these institutions. Marxism, which started as a theoretical framework, slowly morphed into a lens through which everything was analyzed and critiqued. The impact was profound and far-reaching. Students graduating from these institutions carried with them not just a degree, but a worldview shaped by Marxist principles.

This integration of Marxist thought was not limited to the realms of academia. It began to permeate into the wider political and economic spheres. A new political class emerged, one that was distinctly different from the traditional American working class. This class was educated, articulate, and deeply influenced by leftist ideology. They spoke of equality, social justice, and redistribution of wealth, but beneath these noble ideals lurked a more radical agenda—one that sought to upend the very foundations of American society.

The infiltration of Marxism into American higher education was more than just an academic trend; it was a pivotal moment in the political and social evolution of the United States. It signaled a departure from traditional American values of individual liberty, free enterprise, and limited government. Instead, what emerged was a philosophy that favored collective solutions, government intervention, and a skepticism, if not outright hostility, toward capitalism.

This historical emergence of leftism in American higher education was not merely a shift in academic preference. It was a harbinger of a larger ideological battle that would come to dominate the American political landscape. It was a battle between traditional American values and an imported ideology that sought to redefine the very nature of American society.

The legacy of Marxism's entry into higher education is complex and multifaceted. On one hand, it broadened the intellectual horizons of American academia. On the other, it sowed the seeds of an ideological divide that continues to polarize the nation. As we reflect on this historical journey, one question looms large: How will the story of leftism's rise in American society continue to unfold?

## Economic Changes and Leftist Influence

As the tendrils of leftist ideology wound their way through the hallowed halls of academia, a simultaneous and more surreptitious shift was occurring in the economic sphere. This wasn't just about the spread of ideas in lecture theaters and seminar rooms; it reached the very heart of America's financial institutions and policymaking bodies. The result? A profound and perhaps irrevocable alteration in the economic landscape of the nation.

Let's start with a seemingly benign phenomenon: the burgeoning enrollment in higher education. As more Americans sought college degrees, universities expanded both in size and influence. But what was being taught within these institutions was undergoing a transformation. The growing dominance of leftist thought among faculties wasn't just an academic trend; it was a conveyor belt for indoctrination. Students were no longer just learning economics, political science, or sociology; they were being steeped in a worldview that often ran counter to traditional American values of free enterprise and self-reliance.

But the influence of leftism didn't stop at the campus gates. Graduates of these institutions, many imbued with the ideals (or perhaps more accurately, the dogma) of leftism, began to populate key positions in financial institutions, stock exchanges, and, crucially, political administrations. Here, they wielded their influence not through overt activism, but through subtler, yet more profound, means—policy decisions, regulatory frameworks, and economic strategies.

This infiltration into the financial and political realms marked a significant shift. Traditional economic models, which emphasized market freedom and limited government intervention, began to be challenged. In their place, a new model was being proposed, one that favored greater government control, wealth redistribution, and regulation of industries. The ethos of self-reliance and individual entrepreneurial spirit—once the bedrock of American economic success—was being overshadowed by a collectivist approach that viewed state intervention as the solution to economic disparities.

This shift was not merely academic or theoretical. It had real-world consequences. The financial markets, once the bastions of capitalism, began to see an influx of leftist ideology in their practices and policies. It wasn't just about making profits; it was about social responsibility, ethical investing, and other concepts that, while noble in intent, often strayed far from the fundamental principles of market economics.

Meanwhile, in political administrations, the influence of leftist-educated policymakers began to reshape the national economy. Economic policies increasingly reflected a leftist bent, prioritizing social welfare programs, increased government spending, and higher taxes on the wealthy. The mantra became one of equality and fairness, but at what cost? Critics argued that such policies stifled innovation, discouraged entrepreneurship, and led to an overbearing government presence in the daily lives of citizens.

In essence, the economic changes and leftist influence in America represented a paradigm shift. No longer was the American economy purely a tale of capitalism and free markets. It had become a battle-ground of ideologies, where leftist thought challenged traditional economic principles. The question that emerged was profound: Could the fundamental American values of individualism and free market capitalism coexist with the rising tide of leftist economic philosophy? Or was the nation witnessing the emergence of a new economic order, one that would reshape the American Dream itself?

The American landscape, once a tapestry woven with threads of shared dreams and collective aspirations, began to fray under the weight of a divisive ideology—critical theory. This wasn't merely a scholastic debate confined to the esoteric circles of academia; it was the genesis of a profound cleavage in American society, pitting neighbor against neighbor, eroding the very fabric of national unity.

At the heart of this ideological maelstrom was the concept of identity politics, a by-product of critical theory. This wasn't just about recognizing diversity or striving for equality; it became a tool for categorizing, dividing, and setting Americans against one another based on race, gender, and class. The narrative was no longer about the American Dream accessible to all. Instead, it was a story of oppressors and the oppressed, a relentless drumbeat of division and resentment.

But how did this seismic shift come about? It sprang from the soil of higher education, where leftist ideologies had taken root. Here, in the echo chambers of universities, critical theory flourished, indoctrinating a generation with a worldview that saw discrimination and oppression in every facet of American life. This ideology then spilled out beyond the campus grounds, infiltrating the political class—a class increasingly detached from the experiences and values of the traditional American working class.

The divide was stark. On one side were the traditional working-class Americans, whose values were anchored in hard work, community, and a shared sense of national identity. On the other were the proponents of critical theory, who viewed America not through a lens of opportunity and freedom, but through a prism of systemic inequality and injustice.

This ideological chasm was most pronounced in the contrast between urban and rural America. In the cities, where the influence of leftist thought was strongest, identity politics took firm hold, reshaping the political and social discourse. Meanwhile, in rural areas, where the presence of leftist ideology was less pronounced, a different America persisted—one that clung to traditional values and viewed the growing emphasis on identity politics with increasing alienation and distrust.

The division fostered by critical theory and identity politics had another consequence—it reframed the national dialogue around the concepts of democracy and republicanism. Democracy, once a unifying ideal, was being reinterpreted through the lens of leftist ideology. It was no longer just about the rule of the majority; it became a vehicle for advancing the agenda of identity politics. Republicanism, with its emphasis on individual rights and limited government, was increasingly portrayed as an outdated and even oppressive system.

This ideological schism represented more than just differing political views. It was a fundamental reimagining of the American identity. The nation was no longer a unified entity with common goals and shared dreams. It had become a battleground of competing ideologies, each vying to redefine what it meant to be American.

As the nation grappled with this growing divide, the question that loomed large was whether the traditional American values of unity, hard work, and shared destiny could withstand the onslaught of an ideology that seemed intent on tearing them apart. The challenge was clear: Could America bridge this divide, or was it destined to become a nation fragmented by the very theories that sought to redefine it?

## Democracy, Press Propaganda, and Leftist Strategy

In the grand theater of American democracy, a new act was unfolding, one that threatened to rewrite the script of the nation's political saga. This was not a tale of overt conquest or dramatic revolution; rather, it was a story of subtle manipulation and strategic influence. The villains of this narrative? A leftist intelligentsia, adept at leveraging the tools of democracy and press propaganda to steer the course of public opinion and national policy.

The infiltration of leftist ideology into the fabric of American society had set the stage for a sophisticated strategy that aimed to manipulate democratic systems to its advantage. This was democracy, but not as the Founding Fathers envisioned it. It was democracy hijacked by a narrative that skillfully blended truth with ideologically charged propaganda.

The press, once considered the bastion of impartial reporting and a cornerstone of democratic discourse, was co-opted into this strategy. Gone were the days of unbiased journalism; in its place emerged a media landscape that often seemed more intent on shaping public opinion than informing it. This was not the heavy-handed censorship of authoritarian regimes, but something far more insidious—a narrative carefully crafted to align with leftist ideologies, subtly influencing the way Americans thought, voted, and perceived their world.

But the strategy extended beyond the press. The creation of model political parties in America was a masterstroke in this grand design. These were not political parties in the traditional sense, driven by grassroots support and clear ideological lines. They were, instead, instruments of control, designed to channel the political discourse in a direction favorable to leftist ideals. Under the guise of democracy, these parties manipulated the electoral process, presenting voters with a choice that was, in reality, no choice at all.

This strategy was effective, not because it was overt or forceful, but because it was subtle and insidious. It played on the very strengths of the democratic system—freedom of speech, press, and political plurality— and turned them into tools for advancing a specific ideological agenda. The American public, often unaware of the manipulation at play, was caught in a web of propaganda and political maneuvering.

The success of this strategy lay in its ability to present leftist ideology not as an alien or radical force, but as a mainstream, even inevitable, evolution of American political thought. The narrative was persuasive, appealing to ideals of equality, justice, and social welfare, but beneath its veneer lay a more radical agenda—one that sought to reshape the fundamental principles of America.

As this strategy played out across the nation, a question echoed in the minds of those who watched with concern: What was the end-game? Was it a genuine pursuit of a more equitable society, or was it an attempt to consolidate power, to transform America into a state where individual liberties were secondary to the dictates of a leftist ideology?

The implications of this shift were profound. If left unchecked, the very foundations of American democracy—the freedom to think, to speak, and to choose—could be eroded, replaced by a system where dissent was stifled and diversity of thought was a relic of the past.

The challenge, then, was clear: to recognize the strategy at play and to counter it, not with force, but with a renewed commitment to the principles of Americanism and unbiased journalism. The future of America's ideals depended on it.

Amid the tumultuous waves of political and social change, a narrative often overlooked yet crucially important was unfolding: the role of leftism in shaping the trajectory of worker movements. This was not a mere footnote in the annals of history; it was a chapter that revealed much about the strategies and ambitions of leftist ideologies. In the grand chessboard of political maneuvering, leftists positioned themselves not just as players but as kingmakers, influencing the direction of both social democratic and communist movements.

In the gritty reality of labor struggles, where workers sought fair wages and humane working conditions, leftist leadership found fertile ground. They stepped in, not merely as advocates for workers' rights, but as architects of a broader ideological mission. This was about more than improving the lot of the working class; it was about using the worker movements as a vehicle for advancing a radical political agenda.

The influence of leftists in these movements was multifaceted. On one hand, they championed the cause of the workers, giving voice to their grievances and mobilizing support for labor reforms. On the other hand, they steered these movements toward a more radical path, one that often ran counter to the original goals of fair labor practices and workers' welfare. The endgame was not just social reform; it was a complete overhaul of the economic and political system.

But the role of leftists in worker movements was not confined to the fringes of communism or radical socialism. Their influence was also evident in the mainstream political arena. They managed to permeate both Right and Left political parties, subtly embedding their ideologies within the platforms of these parties. This was a strategic masterstroke, allowing them to shape national policy and public opinion from within the established political framework.

The portrayal of leftists in these movements was complex. To their supporters, they were champions of the downtrodden, crusaders against economic inequality and injustice. To their critics, however, they were opportunists, using the plight of workers as a stepping stone to further their own ideological ends. They were seen as manipulators, skillfully wielding the tools of rhetoric and political organization to sow the seeds of division and discontent.

The irony was not lost on observers: leftists, who claimed to fight for the working class, were often accused of being out of touch with the very people they purported to represent. Their leadership in worker movements was marked by a dichotomy—a blend of genuine advocacy for workers' rights and a calculated strategy to use these movements as a means to an ideological end.

As this narrative unfolded, a fundamental question lingered: Were the leftist leaders of worker movements true champions of the working class, or were they merely using these movements as pawns in a larger game of political power? The answer to this question was critical, for it held the key to understanding the true nature and intentions of leftist involvement in worker movements—and, by extension, their impact on the political and economic landscape of the nation.

In the dynamic and often contentious arena of worker movements, a critical and polarizing debate emerges, one that strikes at the heart of the nation's identity and future: populism versus globalism. This is not a mere skirmish over policy nuances or economic theories; it was a fundamental clash of ideologies, each with its own vision for the future of America and its workforce.

On one side of this ideological divide stands populism, with its clarion call for putting America and its workers first. Populists champion the cause of the working-class Americans or "the American class," advocating for policies that prioritize national interests, protect domestic industries, and preserve the cultural and economic sovereignty of the nation. They view the globalist agenda with skepticism, if not outright hostility, seeing it as a threat to the livelihoods of American workers and the integrity of the nation's economic system.

Contrasting sharply with this perspective is globalism, championed by leftist-led worker movements. The globalist approach, with its roots deeply entrenched in leftist ideology, advocates for a borderless world, where labor and capital move freely across national boundaries. This vision is not just about economic efficiency; it is part of a broader ideological agenda that seeks to transcend national identities and loyalties, promoting a worldview that emphasizes international cooperation and integration.

The Marxist theory plays a pivotal role in shaping the globalist stance in worker movements. It is used as a tool to critique the nationalist approach, portraying it as parochial and outdated. Marxists argue that the struggles of workers are not confined by national borders; they are part of a global class struggle against capitalist exploitation. Thus, they advocate for solidarity among workers worldwide, a stance that often puts them at odds with sentiments in favor of individual liberty.

This clash between populism and globalism in worker movements is more than a theoretical debate; it has real-world implications. The globalist approach, with its emphasis on international labor solidarity and open borders, raises concerns about the impact on domestic employment and the erosion of national economic autonomy. Critics argue that this approach benefits multinational corporations and the economic elite at the expense of the average worker, undermining national economies and local communities.

On the other hand, the populist approach, with its focus on protecting domestic industries and controlling immigration, is criticized for being isolationist and potentially xenophobic. Proponents of globalism argue that nationalism was a reactionary stance, ill-suited to the realities of a globalized economy and an interconnected world.

The debate between populism and globalism in worker movements encapsulates a larger existential question: What direction should America take in an increasingly globalized world? The answer to this question is critical, as it will determine not just the future of American workers, but the very nature of the nation's engagement with the global community.

As this debate rages on, it has become clear that the stakes are high. The outcome of this ideological struggle will shape the economic policies of the nation, influence its foreign relations, and define its role in the global economic order. The future of American labor and the nation's place in the world depends on navigating this complex and contentious terrain.

As the ideological battle lines are drawn within America's borders, a larger, more ambitious narrative is unfolding on the global stage—the international spread of leftist revolutions both violent and cultural. This is not a localized phenomenon confined to a single nation or region; it is a global movement, driven by a vision of radical societal transformation that transcends national boundaries.

The leftist revolutionaries, emboldened by their ideological fervor, set their sights far beyond mere national reform. They envision a world cultural revolution, a sweeping overhaul of the global order that will upend traditional power structures and establish a new societal paradigm based on their interpretation of Marxist principles. This is a revolution with an international scope and grandiose goals, aiming to ignite the flames of leftist ideology across continents.

However, the reality of these international leftist revolutions is often at odds with their utopian aspirations. Time and again, these movements, while initially promising liberation and equality, fall short of creating sustainable civilizations. In their zeal to overthrow the existing order, the revolutionaries frequently overlook the pragmatic aspects of governance and economic management. The result is a series of failed states, characterized by economic turmoil, political repression, and social unrest.

The critique of these revolutions is scathing. Leftist leaders are often portrayed as exploiters, using the rhetoric of social justice and equality to seize power, only to become authoritarian rulers who suppress dissent and erode individual freedoms. Far from contributing positively to the societies they claim to champion, these regimes often leave a legacy of impoverishment, division, and disillusionment.

The international ambitions of the leftist revolutionaries are not just about spreading their ideology; they are about challenging the existing global order. They seek to dismantle the systems of capitalism and liberal democracy, which they view as inherently oppressive and exploitative. In their place, they aim to establish a new world order based on socialist and communist principles—a world where the state plays a central role in controlling the economy and directing societal development.

This vision of a global leftist revolution raises alarm bells among those who value national sovereignty, free markets, and individual liberties. The fear is not just that these revolutions would destabilize the nations in which they occur, but that they will have a domino effect, triggering similar uprisings in other parts of the world. The threat is existential—a challenge to the very foundations of the international order and the principles of republicanism and capitalism.

As the world watches the unfolding of these leftist revolutions, a critical question emerges: Can the international community afford to stand by as these movements seek to reshape the global landscape? The answer to this question is fraught with geopolitical implications. It is not just about opposing a particular ideology; it is about defending a world order that, despite its flaws, has ushered in unprecedented levels of prosperity, stability, and freedom.

The challenge, then, is clear: to confront the international ambitions of the leftist revolutionaries not with mere rhetoric, but with a robust defense of the principles that underpin America. The future of international stability and the preservation of national sovereignty depends on the ability of nations to resist the allure of utopian promises and recognize the dangers posed by these global leftist movements.

As the shadow of leftist ideology extends its reach both within the United States and across the globe, a growing chorus of voices are beginning to articulate a deep-seated apprehension. This concern is not merely about differing political opinions or ideological debates; it is a profound alarm over the perceived existential threats posed by leftism to America and the world at large.

At the forefront of these apprehensions is the fear of America falling prey to a fate similar to other nations that have succumbed to leftist influence. The specters of economic stagnation, political upheaval, and social unrest loom large in these cautionary tales. Observers point to failed leftist experiments around the world, where promises of equality and social justice have given way to authoritarian regimes, economic collapse, and the erosion of individual freedoms. The concern is that if left unchecked, leftism could lead the United States down a similar path of decline.

Beyond the domestic implications, the perceived dangers of leftism extend to the international arena. Critics argue that the spread of leftist ideologies, particularly in their more radical forms, pose a threat not just to individual nations, but to the global order. The narrative is that leftism, with its inherent opposition to capitalism and liberal democracy, seeks to undermine the very foundations of the international system. This is a form of economic and political sabotage, a deliberate attempt to destabilize the state and erode the principles of free markets and democratic governance.

The critique of leftism is multifaceted. Economically, it promotes policies that stifle innovation, discourage entrepreneurship, and lead to unsustainable government debt. Politically, it is antithetical to the values of freedom and individual rights, often resorting to authoritarian measures to maintain control. Socially, leftism fosters division and resentment, undermining the social fabric through its emphasis on identity politics and class warfare.

The ultimate fear is that the endgame of leftism is not merely the reform of existing systems, but their complete overhaul. The goal is economic ruin, national disintegration, and global domination. This vision of leftism is a recipe for chaos, leading to the destabilization of nations and societies worldwide.

As these concerns mount, the response from those opposed to leftism is becoming increasingly urgent. The call is for vigilance and action, for a united front to counter the spread of leftist ideologies. The stakes are nothing less than the preservation of the American way of life and the defense of the global order.

The challenge posed by the perceived dangers of leftism is clear: to engage in a robust and informed debate about the direction of the nation and the world. It is a call to reaffirm the principles of liberty, republicanism, and free enterprise, and to resist the allure of ideologies that threaten to undermine these foundational values. The future prosperity and stability of America, and indeed the world, depends on the outcome of this ideological struggle.

In the unfolding drama of American and global politics, the narrative of leftism presents a climax fraught with dire implications. The final aims and consequences of leftism are not mere shifts in policy or governance but portend a radical transformation of society. This is a scenario where the ideological endgame of leftism poses an existential threat to America along with its values and its culture.

The ultimate goal of leftism is nothing less than economic ruin, national disintegration, and global domination. This is not a vision of incremental reform or moderate change; it is an ideological crusade seeking to dismantle the pillars of capitalism, national sovereignty, and individual freedoms.

Economically, the final aims of leftism are widespread financial instability and collapse. The leftist penchant for expansive government control, heavy taxation, and redistribution of wealth has justly been accused of stifling innovation, discouraging private investment, and leading nations down the path of unsustainable debt and economic stagnation. The consequence, as foretold by critics, is a bleak landscape of diminished prosperity and chronic financial crises.

Politically, the consequences of leftism are equally grave. The ideological thrust of leftism is fundamentally antithetical to the principles of liberal democracy. It harbors authoritarian tendencies, undermining the rule of law, and eroding the checks and balances that safeguard individual liberties. The end result is a political system where dissent is silenced, rights are curtailed, and power is concentrated in the hands of a ruling elite.

Socially, the final aims of leftism are to foster division and strife. The leftist focus on identity politics, class conflict, and social engineering is to be blamed for creating a fragmented society, one marred by resentment, polarization, and a breakdown of the communal bonds that underpin social cohesion. The legacy of leftism is a world of fractured communities and eroded national identities.

The global consequences of leftism are no less concerning. The spread of leftist ideologies across borders is a threat to the stability of the international order. It is an attempt to export a revolutionary agenda, undermining sovereign nations and replacing the global balance of power with a new order dominated by leftist principles.

The final aims and consequences of leftism represent a dire warning. It is a call to action, an urgent plea to resist an ideological tide that threatens to sweep away centuries of progress and freedom. The response required is not just opposition but a reaffirmation of the values and principles that have defined the success of nations and the prosperity of peoples. The future depends on recognizing the true nature of leftism's endgame and taking decisive steps to avert its potentially catastrophic consequences.

In response to the perceived encroachment of leftism, a clarion call resonates across the American heartland, heralding the rise of a robust counterforce: Populist Patriotism.

This movement, rooted deeply in the soil of American values and traditions, emerges as the primary bulwark against the tide of leftist ideologies. It is a rallying cry for those who envision a different future for America—one anchored in the principles of national sovereignty, individual liberty, and a resolute defense of the nation's cultural and historical legacy.

Populist Patriotism is more than a political stance; it is a cultural and social phenomenon. It represents a groundswell of sentiment among vast swaths of the American populace, who feel alienated and marginalized by the sweeping changes and progressive narratives championed by the Left. These are individuals who cling steadfastly to the ideals of the American Dream—the belief in hard work, personal responsibility, and the promise of opportunity for all.

This movement calls for a reassertion of American nationalism, not in the sense of isolationism or xenophobia, but as a proud affirmation of the nation's identity and values. It is a stance that champions the preservation of national borders, the importance of lawful immigration, and the primacy of American interests in global affairs. Populist Patriots view the globalist agenda with deep suspicion, seeing it as a threat to the nation's autonomy and the well-being of its citizens.

At the heart of the Populist Patriot's response is a vehement opposition to the leftist critique of American history and its institutions.

This movement seeks to reclaim the narrative of the nation's past, emphasizing pride in America's achievements and a recognition of its role as a beacon of freedom and republicanism. It is a rebuke to the portrayal of America's history as fundamentally flawed and in need of radical revision.

The prospects for America, as envisioned by Populist Patriots, are inextricably linked to the repudiation of leftist ideologies and a return to core American principles. They advocate for policies that bolster economic freedom, limit government intervention, and protect individual rights. This is a vision of a self-reliant, prosperous America, where merit and effort determine success, and where the government's role is to facilitate, not dictate, the lives of its citizens.

Populist Patriots also call for a reinvigoration of civic education, emphasizing the teaching of American history, the Constitution, and the values of citizenship. This is vital in countering the leftist influence in education and ensuring that future generations remain anchored in the principles that have long defined the American ethos.

The Populist Patriot's response is not just a reaction to the present; it is a statement about the future. It is a declaration that the principles upon which America was founded were enduring and nonnegotiable. This movement represents a beacon of hope for those who fear that the nation is veering off its foundational course, providing a path forward that promises to revive the spirit of American exceptionalism and ensure the nation's prosperity and integrity for generations to come.

In this vision, America's prospects are bright, predicated on the belief that a return to foundational values, coupled with a robust defense against the encroachment of ideologies anathema to the American spirit, will usher in an era of renewed strength and unity. The populist movement rises as a testament to the enduring appeal of America's founding ideals and the unyielding resolve of its people to safeguard their nation's legacy and future.

## CHAPTER 11

# INSURRECTION

In a period characterized by unprecedented global challenges, the American political scene has become a hotbed of contention, raising crucial questions about the legal and political justifications used to undermine the administration of President Donald Trump, especially in the context of the COVID-19 pandemic.

Let's first address the whirlwind of changes to the state election processes in response to the pandemic. Critics argue that these alterations, supposedly made in the name of public health, opened doors to potential election integrity vulnerabilities. One must question whether the rapid implementation of these changes, some argue hastily and without thorough vetting, was in the best interest of American Republicanism or an opportunistic maneuver by those opposing the administration.

Then comes the portrayal of the January 6, 2021 event. The mainstream narrative categorizes this as a right-wing insurrection, an assault against the sacred pillars of American democracy. However, this perspective seems to conveniently sidestep a critical analysis of the underlying causes. Discontent and skepticism were not born in a vacuum but were a culmination of prolonged feelings of disenfranchisement and distrust toward the political establishment.

This notion that might makes right, which seems to underpin the relentless persecution of Trump and his associates, merits scrutiny.

The vigor with which the former president and those connected to the events of January 6 have been pursued raises questions about proportionality and the politicization of justice. It's essential to consider if this is a pursuit of truth and justice, or if it veers into the territory of political retribution, a tool to further vilify and ostracize a particular political faction.

The criticisms and legal actions taken against the Trump administration, particularly in the wake of the pandemic, reflect a broader battle within the American political landscape. It's a conflict between traditional establishment power structures and an emerging populist movement, which the Trump administration, for many, came to symbolize. This movement, often dismissed and derided by the mainstream, found a voice in Trump, and its suppression raises fundamental questions about the nature of American freedom of expression.

The legal and political justifications used to critique and counter the Trump administration, especially in response to the pandemic, must be examined through a lens that considers both the immediate and far-reaching implications for America. It's a matter not just of the administration's actions but of the integrity and resilience of the democratic system itself. As we navigate these complex issues, the need for a balanced, principled approach has never been more critical.

Turning the pages of history, we find ourselves confronted with stark examples of illegitimate power grabs that echo eerily in today's political climate. These instances serve not just as historical footnotes but as critical lessons for understanding the current American political saga.

Consider the Soviet revolutionaries. Their seizure of power was cloaked in the promise of equality and justice, but what followed was anything but that. The revolution led to an authoritarian regime under the guise of people's welfare, raising questions about the legitimacy of power obtained through deceit and manipulation. This parallel is alarming when we scrutinize certain factions in modern America, where the narrative of public good is often used to justify actions that fundamentally alter the political and social landscape.

Then there's the case of Béla Kun in Hungary. Kun's short-lived communist regime was marked by radical policies and actions that went against the grain of the nation's historical and cultural values. His failure to gain lasting legitimacy, despite initial control, is a testament to the idea that true authority stems from a genuine alignment with the people's will, not mere seizure of power.

Drawing a parallel to contemporary America, one must ask: Are we witnessing a similar trajectory? The use of political maneuvers that some perceive as undermining traditional values and democratic processes raises the specter of history repeating itself. When power is seized or maintained through means that appear to contradict the foundational principles of a society, the legitimacy of such power is rightfully questioned.

Moreover, the comparison with historical figures like Bismarck, Kemal Pasha, and Mussolini brings an intriguing dimension to this discourse. These leaders, often vilified or revered, were later seen in a different light as their actions brought significant, albeit controversial, changes to their nations. This retrospective understanding of their legacies invites a nuanced view of contemporary political figures. Are we too quick to judge, or are we failing to see the broader implications of their actions for the nation?

In the theater of world history, certain figures stand out, casting long shadows that reach into our present day. Their stories offer a profound perspective on contemporary political events, especially when we consider the actions and perceived legitimacy of current leaders in comparison.

Take Otto von Bismarck, the Iron Chancellor of Germany. His political maneuvers, often seen as Machiavellian, eventually unified Germany and laid the groundwork for it to become a major European power. Bismarck's policies were controversial, his methods sometimes ruthless, but his vision and decisiveness shaped a nation. In modern America, are we witnessing a similar bold, albeit contentious, effort to reshape the national narrative and identity? The comparison begs the question: Will such actions be viewed through a different lens by future generations?

Then there's Mustafa Kemal Atatürk, the founder of modern Turkey. He radically transformed his country, secularizing and Westernizing it, often in defiance of deep-rooted traditions and beliefs. Kemal's actions were divisive, but he is revered today for modernizing Turkey. This example prompts us to consider whether the leaders we now criticize for challenging the status quo may one day be appreciated for their foresight and daring reforms.

And of course, there's Benito Mussolini. This comparison is more contentious, given the negative connotations associated with his regime. Yet, it's instructive to consider how Mussolini initially garnered support by promising to restore Italy's glory and address economic woes. This historical lens offers a critical view of how populist rhetoric can be both mobilizing and misleading. It challenges us to discern between genuine nationalistic fervor aimed at reform and improvement, and mere demagoguery.

In each case, these historical figures were initially met with resistance and controversy. However, their actions were later reassessed as having brought significant, though sometimes problematic, contributions to their nations. Applying this perspective to the current American political landscape, we must ask: How will the actions of today's leaders be judged by history? Will they be seen as visionaries who took necessary, albeit difficult, steps to steer the nation in a new direction, or will they be remembered as figures who overstepped the bounds of their authority?

As we draw these parallels, it's crucial to approach contemporary events with a sense of historical awareness and a recognition that the final judgment of today's leaders may be more nuanced than the current polarized discourse suggests. History teaches us that the impact and legitimacy of a leader's actions often take time to be fully understood and appreciated.

In the unfolding narrative of a nation, the chapters preceding the COVID-19 pandemic in America were marked by a distinctive sense of direction and a robustness in its standing on the world stage. This period, often overlooked in the heat of current political debates, merits a closer examination to understand the dramatic shift in the nation's trajectory post-pandemic.

Before the world was gripped by the pandemic, America was navigating a course that many viewed as a resurgence of its foundational principles. The economy was on an upward trajectory, unemployment rates were at historic lows, and there was a palpable sense of reinvigoration in the national spirit. This era was characterized by policies that prioritized national interests, a stance that sometimes clashed with globalist perspectives but resonated with a significant portion of the American populace.

Furthermore, the pre-pandemic period saw America taking a firm stand in international relations, reasserting its position in global politics. The administration's approach to foreign policy, often criticized for its unapologetic America-first stance, was, in reality, a recalibration toward prioritizing American interests, a concept that resonated with many citizens who felt that the nation's interests had been sidelined in favor of global diplomacy.

In the realm of national security, the narrative was one of vigilance and strength. The administration's policies were aimed at fortifying the nation's borders and enhancing its security apparatus. This approach was a departure from previous administrations and was often at the center of heated debates. However, it reflected a commitment to safeguarding the nation's integrity against perceived threats, both external and internal.

As we reflect on this period, it's essential to recognize the underlying sentiment that propelled these policies. There was a burgeoning movement that sought to rekindle American pride and self-reliance, a movement that found resonance in the administration's actions. This was not merely a political stance but a cultural shift, where the ethos of American exceptionalism and independence was being reasserted.

The pre-pandemic America was not a utopia, and it faced its share of challenges and criticisms. Yet, it was a time marked by a clear sense of purpose and a drive to reestablish the country's standing on the global stage. As we grapple with the pandemic's aftermath and its impact on the nation, understanding this pre-pandemic state is crucial. It serves as a benchmark against which the current state of affairs can be measured and understood, providing a clearer picture of the trajectory that America was on and the shifts that have since occurred.

The narrative has dramatically shifted from the pre-pandemic era's aspirations and achievements to a landscape marred by what many perceive as the failures and overreaches of the political class. This shift has exposed deep-seated issues within the nation's governance, raising significant concerns about abuses of power and broken promises.

The pandemic ushered in a period where the political establishment seemed to diverge from its commitment to serving the populace. Economic strategies, once focused on growth and stability, gave way to policies that many argue led to economic stagnation and insecurity. The promises of prosperity and opportunity were overshadowed by rising unemployment and economic turmoil, issues that were exacerbated, if not directly caused, by the political leadership's decisions during this time.

Internationally, the political class's handling of foreign affairs and conflicts has also come under scrutiny. The shift from a strong, principled stance in global politics to a more appeasing approach has raised questions about the nation's position and influence on the world stage.

Critics argue that this has not only diminished the country's global standing but has also compromised its ability to effectively advocate for its interests and values.

Furthermore, the political instability, marked by deepening divisions and escalating tensions, points to a failure in leadership. Instead of bridging the widening gaps, the political class has been accused of fueling the divide, using partisan tactics to consolidate power rather than fostering unity and consensus. This has led to a polarized and fractured political environment, where cooperation and constructive dialogue have become casualties of partisan warfare.

Perhaps most troubling is the perception of a brazen abuse of power by the political class. The relentless pursuit of certain political figures, the use of intelligence and law enforcement agencies for political ends, and the suppression of dissenting voices are seen by many as a betrayal of democratic principles. These actions have raised alarms about the erosion of civil liberties and the rule of law, foundational pillars of the American system.

The implications of these perceived failures and abuses of power represent not just policy missteps but a deeper crisis in the American political system, where trust in institutions and leaders is eroding. This crisis calls for a critical examination of the role and responsibility of the political class, a reevaluation of their commitment to the nation's principles, and a demand for accountability and reform. The future of American democracy may well depend on how these challenges are addressed and overcome.

In the tumultuous narrative of contemporary America, the concept of national honor, once a cornerstone of the country's identity, has become a subject of intense debate and reevaluation. This concept, deeply rooted in the nation's history, has been brought to the forefront by current events, underscoring a pivotal moment that might well be described as a revolution in the American ethos.

National honor, traditionally, has been synonymous with a sense of pride in the country's achievements, its values, and its global standing. It's about the collective dignity of the American people and the respect accorded to the nation by the international community. However, recent events have led to a questioning of whether the political establishment has upheld or compromised this honor. The narrative being woven by current leaders seems to diverge significantly from the ideals that once defined the nation's sense of self-worth and international repute.

The concept of revolution, in this context, takes on a dual meaning. On one hand, it represents a seismic shift in the nation's political and social landscape, a departure from traditional values and practices. On the other hand, it embodies a call to return to those very principles that seem to be in peril—a revolution not just in policy, but in ideology and national identity.

The idea of preserving national honor has, in many ways, been over-shadowed by a new government's approach that appears to capitulate to external pressures and internal divisiveness. Critics argue that this represents not just a failure in leadership but a betrayal of the American spirit. The erosion of national pride, the wavering stance on the global stage, and the seeming indifference to the values that once defined America's character have stirred a sense of urgency among those who wish to see the nation reclaim its honor.

In this context, the call for revolution is not one of violence or upheaval, but a revolution in thought, perspective, and approach. It's a call for a resurgence of the principles of integrity, courage, and con-viction. This revolution seeks to challenge the status quo, to question the decisions and actions of those in power, and to reignite a collective sense of purpose and pride.

The path forward, as seen by many, is not through further divi-sion or partisanship, but through a recommitment to the ideals that have historically defined the nation. This revolution, grounded in a reinvigorated sense of national honor, may well be the key to navigating the challenges that face America today, steering the nation toward a future that honors its past while boldly embracing the possibilities of the future.

In the current American political landscape, a profound dialogue is unfolding about the role and importance of populist authority. This conversation touches upon the very heart of democracy, questioning the relationship between the governed and their governors. In this era, marked by widespread skepticism toward the traditional political class, the concept of populist authority emerges not just as a political phenomenon, but as a clarion call for a return to the fundamental principles of governance "of the people, by the people, for the people."

Populist authority, often maligned by the mainstream narrative, actually encapsulates the essence of democracy. It represents a form of power that is rooted in the will and the needs of the common people, rather than the elite or the established political order. This populist wave is not an aberration; rather, it is a response to what many perceive as a detachment of the ruling class from the everyday realities and concerns of the average citizen.

In the face of current challenges, the significance of populist authority becomes even more pronounced. It serves as a counterbalance to a political establishment that seems increasingly out of touch with the populace. The rise of populist sentiment is a direct consequence of the failures and perceived betrayals of the traditional political elite. When promises are broken, when trust is eroded, and when the voices of the ordinary citizens are ignored or suppressed, the appeal of populist leaders who promise to challenge the status quo and to represent the "real" voice of the people grows stronger.

However, the current state of populist authority in America is mired in controversy. Its detractors view it as a threat to democratic norms and institutions, while its proponents see it as a necessary disruption to a complacent and unresponsive political system. This dichotomy reflects a broader struggle over the future direction of the country and the nature of its democracy.

The criticism leveled at the current state's lack of legitimacy among those in power underscores a growing disconnect. The essence of populist authority lies in its legitimacy derived from the people. When the ruling class is perceived as serving its own interests rather than those of the public, it loses its legitimacy, and the populist call for change becomes louder and more compelling.

The importance of populist authority in the current American political climate cannot be overstated. It is a manifestation of the democratic spirit, a response to the perceived failures of the political establishment, and a reminder that the true power in a democracy lies with the people. As America navigates these tumultuous times, the role of populist authority will likely continue to be a subject of intense debate and analysis, shaping the nation's political discourse and its future trajectory.

## Patriotism and Populism's Role in America's Future

In the unfolding saga of contemporary America, the interplay of patriotism and populism paints a complex portrait of the nation's future. This era, defined by seismic shifts in the political and social fabric, beckons a deeper understanding of how these twin forces are shaping the destiny of a country at a crossroads.

Patriotism, in its purest form, is an unwavering love for one's country, a commitment to its values and a dedication to its prosperity and well-being. In recent times, however, this noble sentiment has been entangled in the polarized debates that dominate the national discourse. True patriotism, as many argue, is not about blind allegiance to a particular ideology or political figure, but a steadfast devotion to the principles that constitute the American ethos—liberty, justice, and equality.

Populism, on the other hand, has emerged as a powerful force, challenging the status quo and giving voice to those who feel marginalized by the mainstream political system. It speaks to the heart of American democracy, reflecting a yearning for a governance that truly represents the will of the people. This populist wave is not an aberration; rather, it is a manifestation of a deep-seated desire for a political renaissance that reclaims the government for the common citizen.

The narrative of globalism versus Americanism plays a pivotal role in this context. Globalist agendas, as perceived by some, seek to dilute national identity and sovereignty, prioritizing international interests over national ones. In contrast, the populist movement, intertwined with patriotic fervor, advocates for an America-centric approach, emphasizing the need to prioritize American jobs, security, and interests.

The role of the political establishment in this dynamic is critical. Critics argue that the establishment, in its pursuit of globalist objectives, has neglected the very people it purports to serve. This perceived abandonment has not only fueled the populist movement but has also led to a reevaluation of what it means to be patriotic. The protection of American values and interests, many contend, is paramount and should supersede the motives of international dominance or control.

In the future, the interplay of patriotism and populism will undoubtedly be a defining feature of America's political landscape. The call for a reinvigorated American spirit, rooted in populist principles, highlights a desire for a return to a governance that resonates with the everyday struggles and aspirations of the American people.

It's clear that patriotism and populism will continue to play a crucial role in shaping America's future. These forces, reflective of a deep-seated yearning for a government that truly embodies the ideals of democracy, will drive the nation's discourse and decisions. As America navigates the complexities of the twenty-first century, the fusion of patriotic zeal and populist vigor may well chart the course toward a renewed and robust American identity.

Now emerges a clarion call for a reinvigorated American will. This call transcends mere political rhetoric, striking at the core of the nation's identity and its path forward. It is a summons to awaken the dormant spirit of patriotism, to galvanize a populace yearning for direction, and to ignite a movement rooted in the bedrock principles of Americanism.

The essence of this call is a revival of the indomitable American spirit—a spirit characterized by resilience, innovation, and a relentless pursuit of excellence. It's an appeal to rediscover the nation's founding ideals: liberty, democracy, and the unyielding belief in the potential of every citizen. This resurgence of will is not just about reclaiming past glories but about forging a future that upholds these timeless values in the face of modern-day challenges.

Central to this call is the recognition of the role of a strong populist movement. This movement is envisioned not as a divisive force, but as a unifying call to action, rallying Americans across the spectrum to participate actively in the shaping of their destiny. It's a movement that champions the cause of the average citizen, advocating for policies and practices that reflect the collective aspirations and concerns of the American people.

The necessity of this reinvigorated will is underscored by the trials and tribulations that the nation currently faces. From economic uncertainties to social upheavals, the challenges are manifold. Yet, within these challenges lies the opportunity for America to redefine itself, to demonstrate resilience, and to emerge stronger. It is a chance to show that the spirit of America—innovative, indomitable, and inclusive—remains the guiding force in navigating these turbulent times.

This call for a reawakening is not just about political or economic revival; it's about a cultural and social rejuvenation. It's about instilling a sense of pride and purpose in being American, about fostering a society that values hard work, integrity, and community. It's about creating a narrative that celebrates diversity yet finds strength in unity, a narrative where all Americans feel they have a stake in the nation's future.

The call for a reinvigorated American will is a rallying cry for a nation at a crossroads. It's an invitation to every citizen to play a part in shaping a future that is reflective of America's highest ideals. As the nation moves forward, this renewed spirit—powered by the will of its people and grounded in the principles of populism and patriotism—will be instrumental in charting a course toward a prosperous, equitable, and proud America.

As we reach the denouement of this critical chapter in American history, we find ourselves standing at the precipice of historical judgment. This final appeal is not merely a retrospective gaze but a profound contemplation of how the events and decisions of today will be etched in the annals of time. It is an acknowledgment that the true measure of our actions and choices lies not in the immediate reactions of contemporaries but in the considered verdict of history.

In the grand tapestry of history, every epoch is judged by the legacy it leaves behind. The current era, marked by political upheaval and social transformation, will undoubtedly be scrutinized by future generations. They will look back not only at the surface-level events but delve into the depths of the motivations, principles, and consequences that defined these times.

The allegations of treason, the accusations leveled against those who stood against the prevailing political winds, will be seen in a different light by history. Beyond the courtrooms and the media sensationalism, history has a way of uncovering the truth, of stripping away the veneers of partisanship and exposing the core of what really transpired. The individuals currently maligned and vilified may well be remembered as champions of liberty, as defenders of the true American ethos, fighting not for personal aggrandizement but for the welfare and integrity of the nation.

This final appeal to historical judgment is a reminder that the narrative of the present is often incomplete and sometimes skewed. The figures currently cast as villains may yet emerge as visionaries; the events now seen as tumultuous might be recognized as pivotal moments of necessary change. History has a penchant for revealing the broader context, for providing a perspective that is often lost in the immediacy of current events.

As we stand at this crossroads, it is imperative to remember that our actions and decisions will be subject to the unyielding scrutiny of posterity. The judgments we pass, the stances we take, and the leaders we choose to follow or oppose—all these will undergo the rigorous examination of time. This is not a call to fear historical judgment but to embrace it as a guiding principle, to act with the awareness that our choices have consequences that resonate far beyond our immediate horizon.

History is the ultimate arbiter of truth and justice. As we navigate these tumultuous times, our actions must be guided by a commitment to principles that withstand the test of time, principles that align with the enduring spirit of America. Let us move forward with the resolve to make choices that, when judged by history, will be seen as contributing to the betterment and honor of this great nation.

CHAPTER 12

# A DIRE AMERICA

Let's take a hard look at the state of our political system. It's like a grand theater, isn't it? On one side, we have politicians draped in the flag of democracy, assuring us that every election is a step toward a brighter future. But let's pause and ask ourselves: What tangible changes have these elections brought for the average American?

Consider this: in the last few decades, regardless of which party holds power, the lives of the middle class continue to stagnate. Wages are barely budging, jobs are still being shipped overseas, and the cost of living is skyrocketing. So, what exactly are we voting for? Are these elections anything more than a ceremonial gesture, a facade of choice where the real decisions are made behind closed doors by the same set of elites?

Historically, our nation was a beacon of sovereignty and self-determination. Yet, what we witness now are political institutions—that appear to be mere puppets—fulfilling terms set by international treaties and agreements, far removed from the immediate concerns of you and me. Our Founding Fathers established a republic where the government was supposed to be "of the people, by the people, for the people." But ask yourself, when was the last time you felt that your vote truly influenced the direction of this nation?

The effectiveness of our political system is not just in question; it's in crisis. The promise of change is always there, dangled like a carrot in front of us every four years. Yet, the real changes—the ones that matter in our daily lives—remain elusive. It's time to face the uncomfortable truth: our current political system, with its pageantry of elections and the illusion of choice, is failing the American people.

What we need is not just a change of guard but a fundamental shift in how we approach politics. It's not about Left or Right anymore. It's about addressing the needs of the ordinary citizen versus serving the interests of a global elite. The question now is: are we brave enough to demand a system that genuinely represents us, or will we continue to play our part in this elaborate political charade?

The state of our political system is more than just disappointing; it's a dire warning. A warning that if we continue on this path, the very essence of our democracy could be at stake.

Now, let's turn our gaze to an analogy that's as stark as it is true: our great nation, at this very moment, resembles a patient in the grips of a chronic illness. And not just any illness, but one that's been misdiagnosed and mistreated for years by the very people sworn to protect and heal it.

Think about a person suffering from a long-term, debilitating disease. The symptoms are there, clear as day—economic turmoil, social unrest, eroding trust in institutions. Yet, what does the establishment do? They prescribe the same tired treatments: more government intervention, increased spending, and endless political rhetoric. It's like giving aspirin to a patient with a deep, systemic infection. Sure, it might mask the pain temporarily, but does it address the root cause? Absolutely not.

This chronic ailment of our nation is not just an economic downturn or a social issue that can be patched up with half-hearted reforms. No, it's deeper than that. It's a prolonged crisis of identity, purpose, and direction. Just as a chronically ill patient suffers from a lack of vitality, so too does our nation suffer from a lack of vision and true leadership.

Where is the robust, thriving America we once knew? What happened to the ideals and dreams that fueled our growth and prosperity? They've been neglected, forgotten, like a patient wasting away from neglect. The spirit and vigor of our nation are being drained by the very people who claim to be its caretakers.

It's time we realize that this national sickness is not a normal state of affairs. It's an alarming signal that something is fundamentally wrong. And like any responsible doctor, we need to diagnose the problem correctly and treat it with the seriousness it deserves. Not with bandages and platitudes, but with a comprehensive plan to restore the health and vitality of our nation.

In short, America is not just experiencing a rough patch. It's suffering from a deep, systemic illness that requires a radical rethinking of how we approach our politics, our society, and our national identity. And the first step to recovery? Acknowledging that we're sick.

Now, let's draw a parallel that some might find controversial, but it's essential to understanding where we stand today. Think back to the Civil Rights Movement, a pivotal moment in our history. The figurehead of this monumental movement? Martin Luther King Jr., a man who stood against the tide, fighting for a dream that seemed almost unreachable at the time.

Today, we find ourselves at a similar crossroads. The issues are different, sure, but the essence? It's remarkably similar. It's about fighting for the soul of our nation, for the principles that seem to have been forgotten in the haze of political correctness and global agendas.

Martin Luther King Jr. didn't just deliver speeches; he mobilized people, he inspired a nation to look at its ugliest parts and dare to change them. He wasn't about maintaining the status quo or making empty promises. He was about action, about profound change at the grassroots level. Isn't that precisely what we need today? A movement not of words, but of decisive action?

But here's where we need to tread carefully. Drawing a parallel with such a significant figure in American history is not about appropriating his struggle or equating our current issues directly with the monumental fight for civil rights. It's about understanding the kind of determination, unity, and clarity of purpose that's required to bring about real change.

King's movement was about facing hard truths, about challenging an entire system of entrenched beliefs and practices. That's exactly what's needed today—a willingness to confront the uncomfortable, to shake the foundations of a system that's become too complacent, too detached from the real needs of the people.

Let's be clear: this isn't about replicating the past. It's about learning from it. It's about understanding that when the direction of a nation starts to veer off course, it takes more than just politicians and their promises to right the ship. It takes a collective awakening, a movement of people united by a common goal.

In essence, what we're facing today is a call to action, akin to what Martin Luther King Jr. championed. It's a call to wake up, to recognize that the path to true change is not through the same old political charades, but through a renewed sense of purpose, a reinvigoration of those fundamental values that once made our nation great.

Now, let's delve into a dimension of our crisis that's often overlooked but is perhaps the most critical: the spiritual, ethical, and moral decay that's eating away at the fabric of our society. This isn't just about economic downturns or political missteps; it's about a profound loss of direction, a moral compass that seems to have gone haywire.

Think about it. When was the last time our leaders talked about virtues like integrity, honesty, and responsibility? Not as empty buzzwords, but as essential pillars of a thriving society? We're so caught up in the materialistic rat race, in the endless pursuit of wealth and power, that we've neglected the very principles that hold a nation together.

This crisis is more than skin deep. It's a spiritual void, a gaping hole where once there were shared values and a common sense of purpose. We've become a nation of individuals chasing personal gain, forgetting that our true strength lies in our collective character, in our ability to stand for something greater than ourselves.

Ethically, what do we see? A political and corporate landscape riddled with corruption and self-interest. It's no longer about what's right or just; it's about what's profitable or politically expedient. And the moral cost? It's staggering. We're witnessing a decline in social cohesion, an erosion of trust and respect for one another, and the rise of a "me-first" mentality that threatens the very idea of community.

This isn't just troubling; it's alarming. A nation without a strong ethical foundation is like a house built on sand—vulnerable to every wind of change, every tide of adversity. We need to wake up to this reality and understand that rebuilding our nation means more than just economic reforms or political strategies. It means rekindling the spirit of what it truly means to be a part of this great country.

The question we need to ask ourselves is this: Are we willing to look beyond the superficial, to address the deeper spiritual, ethical, and moral issues that are at the heart of our crisis? It's a tough question, but it's one we can't afford to ignore. Because the future of our nation depends not just on the strength of our economy or the soundness of our policies, but on the character of our people and the values we uphold.

The crisis we face is as much a spiritual and moral one as it is political or economic. And the path to healing, to true revival, starts with a return to those fundamental virtues that once made us not just a powerful nation, but a good one.

Now let's face a hard truth about our society—a division so profound, it's tearing at the seams of our nation. We're talking about the great divide between the American working class and the globalist political class. This isn't just a gap; it's a chasm, widening each day, fueled by policies and agendas that seem to have forgotten the average Joe.

On one side, we have the American working class—the backbone of this nation, the hard workers who build, serve, and keep the country running. They're the ones feeling the pinch of every bad policy, every economic downturn. They've been promised change, progress, a better life. But what have they received? Empty promises, factories closing down, jobs slipping away overseas. They feel betrayed, and who can blame them?

On the other side stands the globalist political class—a group more concerned with international agendas than the plight of the American worker. They sit in their ivory towers, crafting policies that serve global interests, talking about a borderless world while the very people they represent struggle to make ends meet. They're disconnected, living in a bubble that's far removed from the day-to-day realities of most Americans.

This division is more than just economic disparity. It's about a loss of identity, a feeling of being forgotten by those in power. The working class sees a political elite that's more interested in serving themselves and their international allies than addressing the issues at home. And let's not forget—both sides of the political spectrum are guilty of this. It's not a Left or Right issue; it's an American issue.

What's worse is that both sides, despite their grandstanding and rhetoric, have failed spectacularly to achieve their political objectives. The working class continues to struggle, and the political class remains out of touch. It's a cycle of disappointment and disconnection, spinning out of control.

It's time we asked ourselves: How did we get here? How did we let this division become so deep, so ingrained? And more importantly, how do we bridge this gap? Because let's be clear—a nation divided against itself cannot stand. We need to start seeing each other not as adversaries, but as fellow Americans, with a shared destiny and a common goal—the prosperity and well-being of our nation.

* * *

This division in our society is not just a political problem; it's a national crisis. And solving it requires more than just lip service from our leaders. It requires a genuine effort to understand and address the needs and concerns of all Americans, not just those who walk the corridors of power.

Let's talk about a group that's been the cornerstone of American society but is now facing an unprecedented crisis—the national middle class. This is the heart of America, folks—the hardworking, everyday citizens who have historically been the driving force behind our nation's growth and prosperity. But what's their reality today? It's a tale of unfulfilled promises and dwindling power.

Once upon a time, the American middle class was the embodiment of the American Dream. They were the homeowners, the community builders, the voters who really mattered. Fast forward to today, and what do we see? A middle class that's shrinking, burdened by taxes, struggling with stagnant wages, and facing a future less bright than the one their parents knew.

Now, why is this happening? Because the middle class has been systematically neglected, if not outright betrayed, by those in power. They've been sold the dream of a powerful, free America, where hard work pays off and fairness reigns. Instead, they've been handed a reality where the deck is stacked against them, where the rich get richer, and the political elite dance to the tune of lobbyists and special interests.

The failure here is twofold. First, there's the failure of the middle class to maintain its role as the stabilizer and innovator of our society. This isn't entirely their fault—they've been hammered by economic policies that favor the wealthy, by trade deals that send jobs overseas, and by a political system that seems more concerned with global affairs than with the plight of the average American worker.

Second, there's the failure of our leaders to protect and empower the middle class. They've paid lip service to the struggles of everyday Americans while enacting policies that do little to improve their situation. The result? A loss of national power, pride, and a sense of direction.

It's high time we asked: What kind of America are we leaving for the next generation? An America where the middle class is a shadow of its former self, struggling to hold on to the basic tenets of a decent life—a stable job, a comfortable home, a hopeful future?

The plight of the national middle class isn't just an economic issue; it's a symbol of a larger problem—the disconnect between the governing elite and the governed. It's a clear sign that our system needs a serious overhaul, starting with a renewed focus on the needs and aspirations of the true backbone of our country: the American middle class.

Now, let's turn our attention to a different yet equally significant issue—the failure of the globalist leftist agenda. This is a story about lofty ideals that promised a utopian world order but ended up far from delivering it. It's about a vision of a socialist, globally interconnected society that, in reality, has not only fallen short but has also led to numerous unintended consequences.

The globalist leftists, with their dreams of a borderless world and a one-size-fits-all approach to governance, have been pushing for policies that, quite frankly, ignore the complexities and unique needs of individual nations, especially our own. They talk about international cooperation and global solutions, but what does that really mean for the average American? It often translates to jobs being outsourced, local industries suffering, and a sense of national identity being eroded.

Their approach has been marked by a focus on materialistic values and a neglect of the deeper, cultural aspects of society. In their pursuit of a so-called progressive agenda, they've overlooked the importance of tradition, community, and a sense of belonging. The result? A fragmented society, where the idea of a united community with shared values and goals seems like a distant memory.

Let's be clear: the stated goals of the globalist leftists—a fair, equitable, and peaceful world—are admirable. But the path they've chosen to achieve these goals is fraught with missteps and miscalculations. Their overemphasis on globalism has come at the cost of national pride and sovereignty. And the worst part? Their failure to achieve genuine social progress has led to increased skepticism and disillusionment among the very people they claim to represent.

So, where do we stand now? We have a globalist movement that's out of touch with the ground realities of the people it claims to serve. A movement that's become more about maintaining a particular political and ideological narrative than about delivering real, tangible results.

The failure of the globalist leftist agenda is not just about unmet promises or misguided policies; it's a stark reminder of the need for a balanced approach that respects national identity and sovereignty while striving for global cooperation. It's about understanding that true progress doesn't come from erasing borders or silencing dissenting voices, but from respecting diversity and fostering a genuine dialogue that leads to practical solutions.

Now, let's dive into a topic that's become somewhat taboo in today's discourse but is crucial to the health and vitality of our nation—the importance of cultural identity and character. In an era where the concept of a melting pot is often replaced with a push toward a bland, uniform global culture, we're losing sight of what makes America truly unique.

Cultural identity—it's the bedrock of any society. It's about shared history, traditions, values, and beliefs. It's what binds us as a community, gives us a sense of belonging, and shapes our character as a nation. But what's happening today? There's a relentless push toward a generic, global identity that undermines the rich tapestry of American culture. This isn't just about preserving heritage; it's about maintaining the very essence of who we are as a people.

And let's talk about character—the moral and ethical qualities that define us as individuals and as a society. These qualities are shaped by our cultural identity. They guide our decisions, our actions, and ultimately, the direction of our country. But in the rush to embrace a borderless world view, are we not risking the dilution of these qualities? Are we not losing the distinctiveness that has long been a hallmark of the American spirit?

The irony is, in the name of inclusivity and global unity, there's an increasing intolerance for the celebration of our unique American culture and values. The very idea of taking pride in our national identity is often painted as outdated or even offensive. But isn't it possible to be proud of one's culture while respecting others? Isn't the true strength of America found in the harmony of its diverse cultural identities and not in the suppression of them?

We're not just talking about preserving cultural artifacts or celebrating traditional festivals. This is about recognizing and valuing the underlying principles that these cultural elements represent—principles like freedom, individualism, and a pioneering spirit. It's about understanding that the character of our nation is intrinsically linked to the preservation and appreciation of our cultural identity.

The erosion of our cultural identity and character isn't a minor issue; it's a major threat to the very fabric of our society. It's time we had an honest conversation about this, recognizing that our strength lies in our diversity and the unique character of our nation. Embracing globalism doesn't mean we have to lose our identity; it means we bring the best of who we are to the global table.

In the midst of all these discussions, let's shed light on a concept that could very well be the antidote to our nation's woes: populist patriotism.

This isn't about blind nationalism or a regressive clinging to the past. No, populist patriotism is about a pragmatic and forward-looking approach that marries national pride with a genuine concern for the welfare of all citizens.

Populist patriotism is a call to return to the core values that made America great in the first place. It's about putting the interests of the American people first, not as an afterthought, but as the guiding principle of governance. This means policies that boost local jobs and industries, that prioritize the well-being of the average citizen over the interests of multinational corporations and foreign entities.

But it's more than just economic policy. Populist patriotism is about reviving the spirit of community, of shared purpose and collective effort. It's about remembering that we're not just a collection of individuals living in the same geographical space; we're a nation, with a shared destiny. It's a recognition that our strength doesn't come from our diversity alone, but from our ability to unite under common ideals and objectives.

Now, there will be naysayers who label this approach as simplistic or nationalistic. But let's be clear—advocating for the interests of your country and its people is the fundamental duty of any government. It's not about closing off from the world; it's about ensuring that engagement with the world benefits the people at home.

Populist patriotism is also a rebuke to the political elite who have long ignored the voice of the ordinary citizen. It's about restoring power to the hands of the people, ensuring that the government is truly of the people, by the people, and for the people. It's a movement that transcends traditional party lines, uniting citizens around a common love for their country and a shared vision for its future.

Populist patriotism isn't a step backward; it's a leap forward. It's a rallying cry for those who believe in the greatness of America, not as an imperial power, but as a beacon of hope, opportunity, and freedom. It's a call for a self-reliant America, resilient in the face of global challenges, proud of its heritage, and optimistic about its future.

Let's bring our discussion to a crucial point, the rallying cry that should echo in the halls of power and in the streets of every American city: the call for a national revival. This isn't just a wishful thinking; it's an urgent necessity. We're at a pivotal moment in our history, where the path we choose will determine the future of our nation for generations to come.

National revival—what does it mean? It's about reawakening the American spirit, reigniting the flames of patriotism, and recommitting to the common good. It's about shaking off the apathy, the disillusionment, and the cynicism that have crept into our national psyche. This revival is a call to action for every American, to remember what we stand for and what we can achieve when we stand together.

It's about sacrifice—not the kind that's forced upon us, but the kind we willingly embrace for the sake of our fellow citizens. It's about understanding that our responsibilities to our country and to one another go beyond just casting a vote or waving a flag. It's about active engagement, about standing up and speaking out for what we believe in.

This call for national revival is also a challenge to the status quo, to the entrenched interests that have long held our political system hostage. It's a demand for genuine change, for policies and leaders that reflect the will and the needs of the people, not just the agenda of the elite.

But let's be clear; this revival isn't about returning to a mythical past. It's about learning from our history, building on our successes, and correcting our mistakes. It's about forging a future that's brighter, more just, and more prosperous than anything we've known before.

This call for national revival is more than just rhetoric. It's a blueprint for a renewed America—an America where unity and purpose replace division and apathy, where the ideals of liberty, justice, and the pursuit of happiness are not just words in a document, but realities in our daily lives. It's an America that we can all be proud of, an America that leads not by coercion or intimidation, but by example.

Now is the time for this revival. Now is the time for us to rise to the challenge. Will we answer the call?

CHAPTER 13

# THE REPUBLIC REBORN

―――――

Imagine an America where the spirit of innovation and freedom ushers in a new era of prosperity and opportunity. This is not a distant dream, but a tangible future that awaits us. In this rejuvenated America, optimism is not just a sentiment; it's a guiding principle.

We are standing at the precipice of a great awakening. Across the nation, a new generation is rising, one that sees beyond the shackles of outdated ideologies and bureaucratic inefficiencies. This generation is ready to reinvent the American Dream, to build a future that echoes the bold ambitions of our Founding Fathers.

In this vision, America reclaims its position as a beacon of hope and progress. Our cities, once stifled by overregulation and mismanagement, bloom into hubs of technological and cultural innovation. The heartland, the soul of our nation, revives with industries that bring jobs back to American soil, championing the dignity of work and the pride of producing American-made goods.

Education becomes a cornerstone of this new era. Schools transform into places where young minds are not only taught but inspired to think critically and creatively. These institutions stand as fortresses against the onslaught of misinformation, producing citizens well-equipped to lead in a world where truth and knowledge are paramount.

The economy in this rejuvenated America is a marvel of the modern world. It's an economy driven by daring entrepreneurship and responsible stewardship, not hindered by overbearing regulations and unfair trade deals. Here, small businesses flourish, unburdened by the heavy hand of an intrusive government, and the American worker is valued and protected.

This is an America where freedom rings true in every corner of society. It's a place where the rights enshrined in our Constitution are not just words on a parchment but are living, breathing principles that guide our daily lives. It's a nation where free speech is celebrated, where religious liberty is revered, and where every citizen has the unalienable right to pursue their own version of happiness.

But this future is not guaranteed. It requires a collective awakening, a national mobilization that calls on each of us to play our part. We must dream boldly, as our forebears did, and act decisively to turn these dreams into reality. The path may be fraught with challenges, but the spirit of the American people has never wavered in the face of adversity.

In this vision for a rejuvenated America, we see a nation reborn, infused with integrity, strength, and an unwavering commitment to justice. It's an America that respects its past, engages with its present, and strides confidently toward a future of unparalleled greatness.

This is the America we can build together, an America where the promise of tomorrow is limited only by the scope of our imagination and the depth of our will to achieve. Let us embrace this vision with the fervor it deserves, for in it lies the blueprint of a nation reborn in the true essence of its founding ideals.

This is a troubling chapter in America's unfolding story we are living right now—a chapter where the very political system that was designed to empower the people has slowly morphed into an unwieldy leviathan, seemingly more interested in serving itself than the citizens it was created to protect.

Our republic, conceived in liberty and dedicated to the proposition of individual freedom, has been gradually and surreptitiously supplanted by a democracy that, in its current form, often seems more like an oligarchy. It's a system where the ideals of fair representation and the sanctity of the individual vote have been eroded by the insidious influence of big money, special interests, and a political elite that appear more concerned with maintaining power than with the welfare of the American people.

Consider this: our Founding Fathers feared the tyranny of the majority and designed a republic to protect individual rights and liberties. Yet, today, we find ourselves in an era where populist rhetoric often drowns out reasoned debate, and significant policy decisions are influenced by the clamor of the moment rather than the enduring principles of justice and liberty.

The transition from a republic to a democracy was meant to empower the people, but in reality, it has opened the door for exploitation and manipulation. The relentless pursuit of power has led to a political landscape where bipartisan cooperation is a relic of the past, and the art of governance is reduced to a perpetual campaign. In this arena, the voice of the average American is lost in a cacophony of political posturing and media spin.

Moreover, the globalist agenda, often hidden beneath the guise of diplomacy and international cooperation, has further compromised our sovereignty. Decisions that significantly impact the lives of everyday Americans are increasingly made in international boardrooms and foreign capitals, rather than in the halls of our own elected institutions. The result? Policies that serve the interests of a global elite, often at the expense of the American worker and the American family.

The symptoms of this systemic malaise are evident: skyrocketing national debt, overreaching regulations that stifle innovation and entrepreneurship, and a foreign policy that too often puts the interests of other nations above our own. This is not the republic our forefathers envisioned. This is not the America that was promised to us.

In this critique, it is essential to remember that the greatness of America lies not in its government, but in its people. The government is a tool, a mechanism for safeguarding the liberties and facilitating the prosperity of its citizens. When it ceases to do that effectively, when it becomes an impediment rather than a catalyst to the American Dream, it is our right, our duty, to demand better.

This chapter in our history need not be the final word. We, the people, have the power to rewrite it. To do so, we must acknowledge the flaws in our current political system and work tirelessly to correct them. We must return to the principles that made America exceptional—limited government, individual liberty, and a relentless pursuit of justice and prosperity for all.

In today's America, the once-esteemed pillars of media and politics stand not as bastions of truth and democracy, but rather as entwined edifices of manipulation and self-interest. This corruption, subtle yet pervasive, has created an environment where the free exchange of ideas and the fundamental principles of our democracy are under siege.

The media, historically revered as the Fourth Estate and a watchdog of the public interest, has largely devolved into a monolithic entity, echoing a singular narrative that serves not the people, but the political and corporate elites. This consolidation of media power has resulted in a disturbing homogenization of thought and opinion, stifling the diversity of perspectives that is the lifeblood of a vibrant democracy. The airwaves and print media are saturated with partisan commentary masquerading as objective reporting, creating a landscape where truth is no longer absolute but rather a variable dependent on political alignment.

This corruption in the media is inextricably linked to the degradation of our political system. The ideal of politicians as public servants has been overshadowed by a reality where many are seen more as agents of special interests than representatives of the people. The once-sacred trust between the elected and the electorate has been eroded by a seemingly endless series of scandals, backroom deals, and a blatant disregard for the principles of transparency and accountability.

The consequences of this dual corruption are profound. In the realm of politics, it manifests as policy decisions increasingly driven by lobbying efforts and campaign contributions rather than the will of the people. In media, it results in a narrative that often obscures and distorts reality, leading to a populace that is misinformed, polarized, and cynical about the very institutions that are supposed to empower and inform them.

One of the most egregious examples of this is the way certain stories are either amplified or suppressed, depending on their alignment with the prevailing narrative. This selective reporting is a disservice to the public and a betrayal of the journalistic ethos. When the media abdicates its responsibility to provide a balanced and comprehensive view of events, it undermines the foundation of our democracy, which is predicated on an informed citizenry.

Moreover, the intertwining of media and politics has given rise to a culture of censorship and self-censorship. Voices that challenge the status quo are marginalized or silenced, not through overt suppression, but through a subtler, yet equally effective, system of social and professional ostracization. This culture of conformity extends beyond the newsrooms and legislative chambers, permeating every aspect of our society, from education to entertainment.

To confront this corruption, it is not enough to merely recognize its existence. We must actively challenge the status quo, seeking out and supporting alternative voices and perspectives. We must demand greater transparency and accountability from both our media and our political representatives. And above all, we must remember that in a democracy, power ultimately rests not with the media moguls or political elites, but with the people themselves.

Only by reclaiming this power, by reasserting our role as engaged and informed citizens, can we hope to cleanse the corruption that has seeped into our media and politics. This is not a task for the faint-hearted, but the stakes—the very soul of our democracy—could not be higher.

As we scrutinize the fabric of our own democratic system, it becomes imperative to cast our gaze beyond our borders, to understand how other democracies around the world fare under similar strains. This comparative lens reveals an unsettling truth—that the pitfalls and para-doxes we face in American democracy are not unique, but rather symp-tomatic of a larger global trend in democratic governance.

Take a moment to consider the European democratic model, often held up as a paragon of liberal values and political stability. Yet, beneath this veneer of civility and progressiveness there lies a stark reality. Many of these nations grapple with the same issues that plague us—political elitism, media bias, and a growing disconnection between the ruling class and the populace. The European Union, for instance, presents a curious case of democratic deficit, where decisions made by unelected bureaucrats in Brussels have far-reaching impacts on the lives of millions, with minimal input from those whom these decisions affect the most.

Further east, the story is no different. Emerging democracies, once bright beacons of hope in a post–Cold War era, now struggle under the weight of corruption, authoritarian tendencies, and the erosion of civil liberties. The democratic process in these nations is often a mere facade, a ritualistic dance around the fundamental issues of governance and representation.

In contrast, consider the nations that have embraced the concept of direct democracy, where the voice of the people plays a more substan-tial role in the day-to-day decision-making process. While this model has its merits, it also comes with its own set of challenges—populism run amok, decision-making paralysis, and the tyranny of the majority, where the rights and needs of the minority are often overshadowed by the will of the masses.

This global panorama of democratic dysfunction serves as a mirror, reflecting our own struggles in the United States. It underscores a fundamental flaw in modern democratic systems: the gradual shift from serving the people to serving the interests of a select few. The core principles of democracy—representation, accountability, and the rule of law—have been compromised, not overtly, but through a gradual process of erosion and neglect.

The lesson here is clear. Democracy, in any form, is not a self-sustaining mechanism. It requires constant vigilance, active participation, and a commitment to preserving its core values against the corrosive influences of power and greed. The challenges we face in America are not a sign of our unique failure, but rather a call to action—a reminder that the preservation of democracy is an ongoing struggle, one that requires the concerted effort of every citizen who values freedom, justice, and the rule of law.

In this context, the American democratic experiment, with all its flaws and failings, still stands as a beacon of hope. It reminds us that while the road may be fraught with challenges, the journey toward a more perfect union is always worth undertaking. It is up to us, as stewards of this legacy, to ensure that our democracy does not become a cautionary tale, but rather a shining example of resilience and renewal in the face of adversity.

Our leaders, who should stand as exemplars of service and integrity, increasingly appear as marionettes, their strings pulled by the unseen hands of global interests and corporate power. The lofty ideals of public service and national interest have been overshadowed by a relentless pursuit of personal and partisan gain. This isn't just a failure of character; it's a systemic betrayal of the trust placed in them by the American people.

Take a closer look at the policies and decisions emanating from our corridors of power. Too often, they seem to align more closely with the interests of multinational corporations and foreign entities than with the needs and welfare of the American citizenry. This alignment raises unsettling questions about where the loyalties of our political leaders truly lie. Are they serving the people who elected them, or are they serving a global agenda that views national borders and the concept of sovereignty as obstacles to be overcome?

In this context, the concept of "globalist leaders" emerges—a cadre of individuals and entities whose allegiance to the idea of a borderless, interconnected world order supersedes their duty to their own nations and people. While global cooperation is undeniably important in our interconnected world, it becomes problematic when it infringes upon national sovereignty and the democratic will of the people.

Moreover, our political landscape is marred by leaders who, rather than confronting and resolving the pressing issues of our times, engage in political theater and divisive rhetoric. This diversion serves a dual purpose—it keeps the public distracted and divided, and it allows these leaders to evade accountability and scrutiny. The result is a populace that becomes increasingly disillusioned and disengaged from the political process, a dangerous trend in any democracy.

But perhaps the most egregious aspect of this betrayal is the way in which it undermines the fundamental principles upon which our nation was built. The United States was founded on ideals of freedom, self-governance, and the rule of law—principles that are rendered meaningless when those in power act in ways that erode these foundations. This betrayal is not just a matter of poor governance; it is an assault on the very essence of what it means to be an American.

It is time to cast a critical eye on our political leaders and the interests they truly represent. It is time for the American people to demand transparency, integrity, and a recommitment to the principles of national sovereignty. Only then can we begin to restore faith in our political system and ensure that our leaders are truly serving the people they were elected to represent.

In the face of a political and media landscape that often seems tilted against the very principles upon which our nation was founded, there comes a time for the American people to stand up, to be heard, and to reclaim the narrative of their own destiny. This is not a call for mere passive observation or armchair criticism; this is a clarion call for active, engaged citizenship.

It's easy to feel overwhelmed by the magnitude of the issues we face, to feel like a solitary voice lost in a cacophony of power and influence. But history is replete with examples of how the determined will of the people has triumphed over the inertia of the status quo. Remember, the very founding of our nation was an act of extraordinary courage and conviction, a testament to the power of collective action in the face of seemingly insurmountable odds.

We must remember that our republic is not a self-perpetuating machine; it requires the fuel of engaged and informed citizenry. Every American has a role to play in this grand experiment of self-governance. It starts with being informed—not just from sources that echo our own views, but from a diverse array of perspectives that challenge our understanding and broaden our worldview.

More than ever, it's essential to exercise the sacred right to vote. Voting is not just a right; it's a duty—an act of commitment to the future of our nation. But our responsibility does not end at the ballot box. Democracy thrives on continuous engagement—attending town hall meetings, writing to elected representatives, participating in peaceful protests, and engaging in community dialogues.

Moreover, this is a call to resist the forces of division and cynicism. In recent times, our national discourse has been marred by an increasing polarization, a tendency to see fellow Americans who hold different views not as fellow citizens but as adversaries. This division serves only those who seek to maintain power by dividing us. Remember, our strength lies in our unity, in our ability to respect and reconcile our differences to forge a common future.

And to the young, the torchbearers of tomorrow, this is your moment. Engage in the political process, bring your ideas and energy to the forefront. Challenge the status quo, but also understand the weight of history and the complexity of the issues at hand. Your voice is not just important; it is essential to the evolution of our democracy.

This call to action is a reaffirmation of our faith in the American spirit—a spirit that refuses to yield in the face of adversity, that rises to meet the challenges of its time with resolve and determination. It's a reminder that the power to shape the future of our nation lies not in the hands of a few, but in the hands of the many.

Let us embrace this responsibility with the seriousness it deserves. Let us engage, debate, and participate with the knowledge that our actions today will shape the America of tomorrow. This is our country, our legacy, and our time to stand up and be counted.

A stark narrative of betrayal has emerged in America, one that cuts to the very heart of our democratic ideals. This betrayal is not of a singular event or scandal, but rather a systemic disillusionment, a growing sense that the political class—our elected representatives—have strayed far from the path of serving the public good, venturing instead into the pursuit of personal gain and power preservation.

This perception of betrayal is not without foundation. Time and again, we witness instances where those in power, entrusted with the sacred duty of representation, seem to act in ways that serve their interests or those of their affluent backers, rather than the needs of the ordinary American. They parade on the national stage, often more concerned with political theater and partisan point-scoring than with addressing the pressing issues that face the average citizen.

But the betrayal runs deeper than just policy missteps or political pandering. It's in the way the political class has seemingly insulated itself from the consequences of its actions. They live in a bubble of privilege and power, disconnected from the daily struggles and concerns of those they are meant to represent. It's a world where accountability seems a foreign concept, and where the rules that apply to ordinary Americans seem not to apply to them.

This disconnect is further exacerbated by the revolving door between politics and big business, where political influence is a currency traded for lucrative positions and consulting gigs. It's a system that breeds cynicism and distrust, where the line between public service and self-service becomes increasingly blurred.

The ramifications of this betrayal are profound. It erodes the very foundations of our democratic system—trust and belief in the efficacy of our institutions. When people feel that their leaders no longer represent their interests, it leads to a breakdown in civic engagement, a sense of helplessness and apathy that threatens the lifeblood of democracy itself.

The narrative of betrayal also fuels a dangerous polarization. As trust in the political class dwindles, people turn to extremes, seeking solace in ideologies that promise simple solutions to complex problems. The middle ground, once the fertile soil for compromise and progress, becomes a no-man's land, scorched by the fiery rhetoric of the fringes.

Yet, in this narrative of betrayal, there is also a call to action. It is a reminder that in a democracy, power ultimately resides not in the hands of the few, but in the hands of the many. It is up to us, the people, to hold our leaders accountable, to demand transparency and integrity in our political processes, and to actively participate in the shaping of our national destiny.

The perceived betrayal by the political class is not just a challenge to be overcome; it is an opportunity to reengage with the democratic process, to remind ourselves that the strength of our nation lies in our collective ability to effect change. It's a chance to restore faith in the idea that our government is of the people, by the people, for the people—and that it should serve no other interest above that sacred trust.

In the unfolding drama of our nation's political and social life, there is one truth that stands resolute, a beacon of hope in the midst of tumultuous times: the true power of America rests not in the marbled halls of Washington but in the hands of its people. This is the unshakeable foundation upon which our nation was built, and it is the American people who are the custodians of its future.

In every corner of this great land, from the bustling streets of our cities to the quiet roads of our rural heartland, lies the real strength of America. It is in the hands of the hardworking men and women, the small business owners, the teachers, the community leaders—these are the architects of our destiny. Their everyday decisions, actions, and beliefs shape the fabric of our society more than any legislation passed in the corridors of power.

Yet, there seems to be an orchestrated effort to diminish the role of the average American in the national narrative. We are told to leave it to the experts, to trust the decisions made by those at the top, as if the common citizen lacks the wisdom or the insight to understand what's best for them. This patronizing view is not only condescending, but it also undermines the very principles of self-governance and individual liberty that are the hallmarks of our democracy.

The truth is, the greatness of America has always sprung from the collective spirit and the unwavering resolve of its people. It is the farmer who rises before dawn, the teacher who inspires young minds, the soldier who defends our freedom—these are the true guardians of the American legacy. Their daily acts of courage, kindness, and conviction are the threads that weave the tapestry of our nation's history.

In this crucial moment, as we stand at the crossroads of history, the role of the American people has never been more vital. It is time for each of us to step up, to engage in the civic life of our nation with renewed vigor. This means being informed, staying vigilant against the forces that seek to undermine our liberties, and participating actively in the democratic process.

It also means fostering a sense of community and shared purpose, reaching across the divides of ideology, geography, and background to rediscover the common values that unite us as a nation. We must remember that our strength lies not in uniformity, but in our diversity, in the rich tapestry of cultures, beliefs, and ideas that make up the American mosaic.

The emphasis on the American people's role is not just a philosophical ideal; it is a practical call to action. It is a recognition that the solutions to our nation's challenges will not come solely from the top down, but from the bottom up, from the collective wisdom, creativity, and determination of the American people.

So let us rise to this challenge, with the knowledge that our actions today will shape the America of tomorrow. Let us embrace our role as the true stewards of our nation's destiny, with the courage to forge a future that reflects the best of who we are, and all that we can become.

Amid the noise and clamor of our divided political landscape, there is a burgeoning vision for a new political movement—a movement not rooted in the entrenched ideologies of the past, but born from the genuine needs and aspirations of the American people.

This vision speaks to a growing sentiment among the populace—a yearning for a politics that transcends the tired dichotomies of Left and Right, Democrat and Republican. It calls for a movement that is not defined by party lines or political affiliations, but by a shared commitment to the principles of liberty, justice, and the unwavering pursuit of the common good.

Imagine a movement that genuinely represents the ordinary American, not as a mere electoral demographic, but as the lifeblood of the nation. A movement that listens to the voices of the small-town business owner, the urban teacher, the midwestern farmer, and the southern veteran—voices that have been drowned out in the current cacophony of political discourse.

This new political movement is not an exercise in utopian idealism, but a pragmatic response to the clear and present need for change in our political system. It is a movement grounded in the reality of the American experience, one that understands the complexities and challenges of our times, but is not paralyzed by them.

The core of this movement is a return to the fundamental values upon which our nation was founded—the values of individual freedom, personal responsibility, and a government that serves the people, not the other way around. It's about reclaiming the narrative of American politics from the hands of the few and placing it back into the hands of the many.

This vision is not about creating another political party in the traditional sense. It's about forging a new path, a third way that breaks the stranglehold of the existing political structure. It's about building a grassroots movement, one that harnesses the power of technology and social media to connect, mobilize, and empower citizens across the country.

But let's be clear, the road ahead for this movement is not an easy one. It will face opposition from the entrenched powers that benefit from the status quo. It will require courage, resilience, and an unshakeable belief in the cause. Yet, the challenges it faces are also its greatest strength. In striving against these obstacles, the movement will forge its identity, galvanize its supporters, and demonstrate its commitment to real and lasting change.

The vision for this new political movement is, at its heart, a call to restore the promise of America—a promise that every citizen has a voice in the shaping of our national destiny, that every individual has the opportunity to achieve their dreams, and that our government reflects the best of who we are as a people.

It's time for a new chapter in the American political narrative, one where the people take back the pen and write their own story. This is the vision for a new political movement—a movement of the people, by the people, for the people. Let us embrace this vision with the passion and determination it deserves, for in it lies the hope of a renewed and revitalized America.

As we stand at the crossroads of our nation's history, reflecting on the tumultuous journey we have embarked upon, one thing becomes abundantly clear: the path to a brighter, more prosperous America lies not in the hands of the few, but in the collective will and action of the many. The chapters we have traversed together in this discourse are not just a reflection of our present struggles but a clarion call to a future filled with possibility and hope.

In envisioning this future, we must not lose sight of the enduring principles that have guided our nation through its darkest hours and its brightest days. Principles of liberty, justice, and the unyielding pursuit of truth. These are not mere words etched into the annals of history; they are the living, breathing essence of what it means to be an American.

The journey ahead will not be without its challenges. We will face opposition, skepticism, and moments of doubt. But let us remember that the greatest achievements in our history were not born from complacency or resignation, but from the relentless spirit of perseverance and the courage to confront the status quo.

The vision for a renewed America, one that returns to its founding ideals and embraces the untapped potential of its people, is within our grasp. It requires us to stand up, to raise our voices, and to take action. It calls for a new breed of leadership, one that is not beholden to the whims of special interests or the allure of political power, but is reso-lutely committed to serving the people.

This is not just a vision for a new political movement; it is a vision for a new era of American greatness. An era where our government is a reflection of the best of who we are, not a reminder of what we aspire to overcome. An era where every citizen, regardless of background or belief, has an equal stake in the future of our nation.

Let us hold fast to the belief that the truths we hold to be self-evident are not relics of a bygone era, but guiding stars for our journey ahead. Let us be inspired by the unwavering belief that our best days are not behind us, but are yet to come. And let us move forward with the conviction that, in the end, truth and justice will prevail, for they are the very bedrock upon which our nation stands.

This is our charge, our duty, and our privilege as citizens of this great nation. Together, let us embrace the task at hand with the fervor and dedication it deserves. For in doing so, we do not just write the next chapter in our nation's history; we secure the promise of America for generations to come.

CHAPTER 14

# A PLACE AND A PEOPLE

Immigration stands as a defining thread in the American story, intricately woven into the fabric of our national identity. Yet, in recent years, this topic has transformed from a rich narrative of diversity and opportunity into a contentious battleground, polarizing our great nation.

At the heart of this debate lies a fundamental question: What does it mean to be American in the modern era? For generations, the United States has been seen as a beacon of hope, a land where dreams are not just pursued but realized. The Statue of Liberty, standing tall with her torch of freedom, has welcomed millions seeking a better life. However, today's America faces a crossroads, challenging the very ethos of our immigration narrative.

Critics of the current immigration system argue that the nation's generosity and openness have been exploited. They point to a litany of issues, ranging from economic strains to cultural clashes, painting a picture of a country losing its essence. A common argument is that we must continuously reassess who we let in, ensuring that their values align with the American spirit—a spirit defined by hard work, resilience, and patriotism.

The narrative that America must forever keep its doors wide open is being questioned. Critics ask, "At what cost?" They highlight the strain on resources, the competition for jobs, and the cultural shifts that large-scale immigration can bring. This perspective posits that a nation without borders and without a clear immigration policy is like a house with no walls—vulnerable and exposed.

In this climate of debate, it's crucial to distinguish between the humanitarian role of America and the need to protect its interests. This doesn't mean closing the doors on the needy and the oppressed; rather, it's about finding a balance. A balance that ensures the sustenance of the American Dream, not just for those who arrive at our shores but also for those who have called this land home for generations.

As we delve deeper into the multifaceted issues surrounding immigration, we must do so with a clear-eyed view of reality, unclouded by political correctness or ideological dogma. It's about asking the hard questions, not shying away from uncomfortable truths, and facing the challenges head-on.

Thus, as we embark on this exploration of immigration and its impact on our national identity, let's do so with the goal of fostering a dialogue that's both meaningful and constructive. A dialogue that respects the past, addresses the present, and looks to the future with a vision that upholds the values and interests of America.

When we speak of immigration, it's not just about the movement of people across borders, but also the movement of wealth—and this brings us to the critical, often overlooked issue of remittance. Remittance, the act of immigrants sending money back to their home countries, might seem at first glance a harmless, even commendable practice. It speaks to the human spirit of generosity, the desire to support families and communities left behind. However, when we examine the broader implications for the American economy, a more complex and concerning picture emerges.

Each year, billions of dollars are siphoned from the US economy through remittance. This is not pocket change; it's a substantial outflow of wealth, wealth that could otherwise circulate within our economy, bolstering local businesses, creating jobs, and contributing to public funds through taxes. Instead, this money exits our borders, often never to return.

The question then arises: How does this exodus of capital affect the average American? Imagine a scenario where every dollar earned here, instead of contributing to our economy, is sent overseas. This means less money spent in local shops, fewer jobs created by local businesses, and a diminished tax base, which in turn impacts public services and infrastructure. It's a domino effect that touches every corner of our society.

Some argue that remittance is a private matter, a personal choice. While respecting individual freedoms is a cornerstone of our democracy, we also need to consider the collective impact of these private choices on our national economy. It's not just about personal decisions; it's about the economic health and security of our nation.

Moreover, the remittance phenomenon raises a fundamental question about loyalty and commitment. When individuals earn their livelihood in the United States but send a significant portion of their earnings abroad, it begs the question: Where do their economic loyalties lie? Are they contributing to the American economy, or are they inadvertently undermining it?

The proposal to ensure that money earned by immigrants is invested in the American economy isn't about curbing generosity or severing familial ties. It's about striking a balance between personal responsibility and national economic health. It's about fostering a system where those who benefit from the opportunities provided by the United States also contribute their fair share to its prosperity.

In addressing the problem of remittance, we are faced with a choice: continue to overlook the issue, allowing billions of dollars to leave our economy each year, or take a stand for the economic well-being of our nation. The path we choose will have profound implications, not just for our current economic situation, but for the future prosperity of America.

As we navigate the turbulent waters of the immigration debate, we must confront an issue that's often shrouded in controversy and emotion: the relationship between crime and immigration. This is a topic that demands our attention, not because it's sensational, but because it's critical to the safety and security of our communities.

Let's start by acknowledging a hard truth: there are criminal elements within every segment of society, and immigrants are no exception. The narrative spun by some, that immigrants are either universally saintly or universally nefarious, is not just oversimplified; it's dangerously misleading. What we seek here is not hyperbole, but facts.

Statistics show a mixed picture. In some areas, immigrant communities exhibit lower crime rates than native-born populations. However, there are also instances where the opposite is true, where certain types of crime are disproportionately associated with immigrant groups. Ignoring these facts does a disservice to the debate and, more importantly, to the victims of these crimes.

The issue becomes even more pressing when we consider illegal immigration. Illegal immigrants, by virtue of their status, often operate outside the bounds of legal oversight. This can create enclaves where crime can flourish, shielded from the reach of law enforcement. The consequences of this are real and palpable, affecting both immigrant and native communities alike.

What's needed is not fear mongering, but a rational and effective approach to the problem. This includes strict screening processes for immigrants to identify potential criminal backgrounds. It also means enforcing our laws, both against those who commit crimes and those who enter the country illegally.

But enforcement alone isn't enough. We must also address the root causes that drive people to commit crimes, whether they're immigrants or native-born. This includes tackling issues like poverty, lack of education, and social marginalization. It's a complex solution for a complex problem, but it's the only way to ensure long-term safety and stability.

In calling for stricter screening and enforcement, the goal is not to cast aspersions on immigrants as a whole. Rather, it's to protect the integrity of our immigration system and the security of our nation. It's about ensuring that those who come to our shores are here to contribute positively to our society, not to undermine it.

A pivotal aspect of the immigration debate is often overshadowed: the need for selective immigration policies. This isn't about exclusion for exclusion's sake; it's about prudence and prioritizing the national interest. It's about ensuring that those who join our American family add value, contribute positively, and align with the ethos that has propelled this nation to greatness.

The current immigration system, mired in bureaucracy and outdated criteria, is failing us in many ways. It often overlooks the most crucial aspect: the quality of individuals we are admitting. The United States, like any sovereign nation, has not only the right but the duty to choose its new members with discernment. This isn't a radical concept; it's common sense, practiced by nations around the world.

What does it mean to be selective? It means prioritizing immigrants who bring skills, talents, and values that complement our society. It means welcoming the best and the brightest: innovators, thinkers, doers, people who can help propel our economy forward, enrich our culture, and participate actively in our democracy. This approach isn't just beneficial; it's essential in an increasingly competitive and complex global landscape.

This policy is not about closing the door on diversity. On the contrary, it's about enriching our nation with diversity that matters— diversity of skills, ideas, and aspirations. It's about looking beyond mere numbers and quotas, focusing instead on the potential contributions each individual can make.

Let's consider the success stories—immigrants who have come to the United States and made remarkable contributions in science, technology, business, and the arts. These stories underscore the immense potential benefits of a well-crafted selective immigration policy. But for every success story, there are countless others who struggle to integrate, who fail to contribute to our economy, or who burden our social systems. This is the harsh reality we must confront.

Streamlining the immigration process for skilled and talented individuals is not just about benefiting America. It also benefits immigrants. By ensuring they can succeed and contribute, we are not setting them up for failure but for a fruitful symbiosis with our society.

Advocating for selective immigration policies is not a stance against immigrants; it's a stance for a stronger, more prosperous America. It's about ensuring that each new American can stand tall, not just on the shoulders of giants who came before, but as giants themselves, ready to carry forward the legacy of this great nation.

In the ongoing conversation about America's future, one aspect that demands our attention yet often slips under the radar is the concept of foreign exchange education. At its core, this practice involves sending American students abroad for part of their education. While the intention might be to broaden horizons and foster international understanding, we must pause and ask ourselves: What are the real implications of this trend for our nation?

The critical issue here is not the exchange itself, but what we are exchanging. Are we inadvertently trading away our pride and confidence in the American education system? Are we suggesting that the key to a robust, well-rounded education lies beyond our shores, in foreign classrooms and campuses? This is not just a matter of national pride; it's a question of national priority and resource allocation.

Consider this: each year, countless dollars, resources, and talents are exported as our students head overseas. These resources could be channeled into enhancing our own educational institutions, into programs that foster innovation, research, and learning right here on American soil. By focusing inward, we have the opportunity to create a system that not only rivals but surpasses international standards.

This isn't an argument against global awareness or cultural exchange. These are valuable, and necessary, aspects of education. However, they should not come at the expense of our domestic educational establishments. It's about balance—ensuring that our students are grounded in an American educational experience that is second to none.

Let's consider the message we send to the world when we imply that the best education can only be found elsewhere. It's a message that undermines our institutions, educators, and ultimately, our students. Why should the world believe in American education if we appear not to believe in it ourselves?

Eliminating foreign exchange education programs isn't about isolationism. It's about investing in American education—in our schools, colleges, and universities. It's about building a system that draws the world to us, not one that sends our future leaders away.

The call to focus on strengthening our educational institutions is a call to invest in America's future. It's about creating an education system that not only competes on the global stage but sets a new standard for excellence. It's about ensuring that the next generation of leaders, innovators, and thinkers are shaped by the best that America has to offer.

It's paramount to reiterate the core message that has underpinned each argument: the urgent need for pragmatic and thoughtful immigration reform. This is not about stoking divisions or pandering to base instincts; it's about confronting reality with eyes wide open and addressing the challenges that face our nation with the seriousness and diligence they deserve.

Throughout this discussion, we've navigated the turbulent waters of remittance, crime, selective immigration policies, and foreign exchange education. These are not topics for the fainthearted; they are complex, contentious, and deeply impactful. Yet, shying away from these discussions is a disservice to the very essence of democracy and to the principles upon which this nation was built.

The United States stands at a crossroads, a moment in history where the decisions we make will not only define the present but will echo through the annals of time, shaping the America of tomorrow. We must ask ourselves: What kind of America do we want to leave for our children? Do we envision a nation that remains true to its ideals of freedom, opportunity, and justice? Or do we risk descending into a quagmire of unmanaged challenges and unresolved issues?

The call for immigration reform is, at its heart, a call for the preservation and enhancement of the American Dream. It's a recognition that while our doors should remain open, they must not be unguarded. We must welcome those who seek to contribute positively to our society, while also safeguarding our citizens' interests, security, and well-being.

The United States, a country with a vast expanse of land stretching from sea to shining sea, has always had a unique relationship with its territory and the people who inhabit it. Historically, the strength and influence of a nation have been closely tied to its population and territorial extent. From the Roman Empire to the British Empire, the expansion of territory and effective population management have been pivotal in their rise to global prominence. In the context of the United States, the pioneering spirit, manifested through westward expansion, was not just about acquiring land; it was about entwining the destiny of the nation with its geographic reach.

Today, this dynamic presents itself in a different light. The question of how we manage our population—who we let in, who we encourage to stay, and how we integrate them into the American fabric—is more crucial than ever. It's not just a matter of numbers; it's about how these numbers translate into economic power, cultural influence, and geopolitical strength.

The relationship between population and territory in the modern era is intrinsically linked to the concept of power. Power in terms of economic might, military strength, and cultural influence. The United States, with its diverse and populous society, coupled with its vast and resource-rich land, has long held a position of global dominance. However, this status is not a given; it requires careful stewardship of both our people and our land.

The challenge before us is twofold: first, how do we maintain and enhance the symbiotic relationship between our population and our territory in a way that ensures continued prosperity and influence? Second, how do we navigate the global stage, where territorial disputes and population movements increasingly dictate international relations and power dynamics?

In essence, the way we handle the interplay between population and territory will significantly determine our nation's future trajectory. It's about understanding that our land is more than just space—it's a resource, a responsibility, and a reflection of our national identity. And our population is more than just numbers—it's a tapestry of talents, ideas, and potential that can drive us forward or hold us back, depending on how well we manage it.

In the discourse on what constitutes the true strength of a nation, a crucial element often gets eclipsed by more tangible metrics like economic output or military might. This element is the internal strength of a nation, a composite of the character, values, and resolve of its people. It's an intangible yet indispensable asset, and its significance in shaping a nation's destiny cannot be overstated.

When we talk about internal strength, we're delving into the realm of national identity, cultural values, and collective will. These are the pillars that support a nation through turbulent times and propel it forward in periods of peace and prosperity. It's about the collective spirit that defines a nation: the resilience in the face of adversity, the shared commitment to common ideals, and the unyielding pursuit of greatness.

Let's bring this concept closer to home. The United States, a country forged from a revolutionary spirit and built on the principles of freedom and democracy, has long demonstrated a remarkable internal strength. From the pioneers who braved the unknown to settle new lands, to the innovators and entrepreneurs who drive our economy, the American spirit has been characterized by boldness, ingenuity, and a relentless drive to succeed.

However, in our current time, we must confront the question: are we losing sight of these intrinsic values? In an age of rapid globalization, where cultural lines are blurred and national identities are challenged, there is a growing concern that we are drifting away from the core values that have defined and strengthened us.

The importance of internal strength is particularly salient when we consider the global landscape. Nations that have maintained a strong sense of identity and purpose have navigated the complexities of the modern world with greater success. Conversely, those that have allowed their internal strength to wane have often found themselves adrift, struggling to maintain cohesion and direction.

It's not just about preserving traditions or holding on to the past; it's about fostering a sense of purpose and unity that transcends individual differences. It's about cultivating a national character that values hard work, innovation, and a commitment to the common good. And it's about ensuring that these values are not just remembered, but lived and breathed by every citizen.

The internal strength of a nation is its bedrock, the foundation upon which all else is built. As we look to the future, we must recommit ourselves to nurturing this strength, to fostering an environment where our values are not just taught, but exemplified in our actions and policies. This is how we ensure that the United States continues to be a beacon of hope, resilience, and unwavering spirit on the global stage.

The topic of the state of political and social unity cuts to the core of our national discourse, raising profound questions about the cohesion and direction of our society. In an era marked by deepening divisions and escalating partisan conflict, the quest for unity is more than a lofty ideal—it's an imperative for the survival and flourishing of our nation.

The concept of unity does not imply uniformity of thought or an absence of disagreement. Healthy debate and diversity of opinion are hallmarks of a vibrant democracy. However, there's a stark difference between constructive disagreement and the fractious, polarized climate that currently characterizes our political landscape. We've reached a point where political affiliations are not just differences in policy preference but chasms that divide friends, families, and communities.

Historically, nations have often found unity in the face of external threats or common enemies. This phenomenon, while effective in rallying a population, is a double-edged sword. It can lead to a temporary cohesion, but it's also a strategy fraught with risks, potentially leading to the demonization of "the other" and the justification of extreme measures in the name of unity.

The current predicament of our political system reveals a glaring absence: a unifying vision that transcends partisan lines and speaks to the common aspirations and values of the American people. The failure of our political parties to provide this vision is not just a failure of leadership; it's a failure to grasp the essence of what makes a nation strong.

Political and social unity should be rooted in a shared commitment to the principles that define us: liberty, justice, and the pursuit of the common good. It's about rediscovering the American narrative, one that speaks to every citizen regardless of political affiliation, race, or creed. It's about forging a path forward that celebrates our diversity while reaffirming our collective identity and purpose.

The pursuit of political and social unity is not a call for mere conformity. It's a call for a renewed sense of purpose and direction, grounded in our foundational values and aspirations. As a nation, we need to move beyond the divisive rhetoric and zero-sum politics that have come to define our era. We need to build bridges where there are currently walls, fostering a spirit of cooperation and mutual respect. This is the path to a stronger, more united America.

As we stand at the precipice of a new era, it is time for a resolute pledge and a clear vision for the future of this great nation. This is not merely a concluding remark in a debate, but a solemn vow to uphold the values and principles that define the American spirit. It's a commitment to steer our country toward a destiny that befits its legacy.

Our pledge is to the timeless ideals of liberty, justice, and the pursuit of happiness. These are not just lofty words etched in the annals of history; they are the guiding stars of our daily endeavors and national policies. It's a promise to uphold these principles in the face of adversity, to defend them against apathy and division, and to embody them in our actions as individuals and as a nation.

But a pledge without a vision is like a ship without a rudder—directionless and destined to founder. Our vision for America is one of renewed strength and unity. It's a vision of a country where the American Dream is not a relic of the past, but a living, breathing reality for every citizen. It's a future where our national discourse is marked not by divisiveness but by a collective pursuit of the common good.

Envision a future rally, not one marked by protest and dissent, but by celebration and unity. Picture a gathering of Americans from all walks of life, different in their backgrounds but united in their purpose. Imagine a scene where the flag is not a symbol of division, but a banner under which we all stand proudly, a symbol of our shared values and aspirations.

This vision calls for sacrifice—not the sacrifice of our values or principles, but the sacrifice of our egos and partisan biases. It demands that we put aside our differences and work together toward a common goal. This is not the sacrifice of compromise; it's the sacrifice of contribution, where each of us adds to the strength and prosperity of our nation.

Our final pledge must be to each other, as citizens of this great country. It's a pledge of respect, cooperation, and shared responsibility. It's a commitment to write the next chapter of our nation's history with the ink of unity and progress. Let this pledge be our guiding light as we navigate the challenges ahead, and let our vision inspire us to build an America that is stronger, more united, and more prosperous than ever before.

## CHAPTER 15

# GLOBALISM AND SOVEREIGNTY

---

Two concepts stand in stark contrast, yet remain inextricably linked: globalism and sovereignty. The journey of the United States, a beacon of freedom and self-governance, through the murky waters of globalism, is not just a narrative of diplomacy but a saga that questions the very essence of national identity and autonomy.

Globalism, a term that has gained prominence in recent decades, refers to the increasing interconnectedness and interdependence of nations, primarily in economic, cultural, and political spheres. It promises a world without borders, a global village where ideas, goods, and people could move freely, fostering an era of unprecedented prosperity and understanding. But, as the curtain rises on the global stage, the reality appears far more complex and, perhaps, less idyllic.

For the United States, a nation built on the pillars of freedom and individual rights, the foray into globalist agendas has been met with both triumphs and challenges. On one hand, globalism has opened markets, spread democracy, and connected cultures. On the other, it has raised questions about the cost to American sovereignty—the ability of the nation to govern itself, free from external influence and control.

The perceived negative impact on American sovereignty cannot be overstated. This is not merely about the loss of control over trade policies or diplomatic decisions. It's about the core of what it means to be a sovereign nation. Sovereignty is the bedrock of a nation's identity, the foundation upon which its values, policies, and traditions stand. It's about having the final say over the laws that govern the people, the security of borders, and the preservation of a cultural heritage that has been nurtured over centuries.

As we delve deeper into this discussion, it's crucial to understand that the narrative is not black and white. The globalist agenda, spearheaded by entities like the World Economic Forum, NATO, and the United Nations, is often painted in a utopian light—striving for a world of cooperation, peace, and shared prosperity. However, beneath this facade of unity and collaboration lies a complex web of power dynamics, where national interests often get sidelined in favor of a broader, sometimes ambiguous, global agenda.

Thus, the crux of our journey through this chapter lies in unraveling the intricate relationship between globalism and American sovereignty. We will explore how the United States, a nation that once held the reins of its destiny firmly in its hands, navigates the challenging terrain of global politics, where every step toward international cooperation can sometimes feel like a retreat from its sovereign legacy. This is not just a discourse on policy or economics; it's a dialogue about identity, self-determination, and the enduring quest of a nation to find its place in an ever-globalizing world.

In the grand narrative of globalism, a narrative often spun with threads of economic integration and cultural exchange, there lies a darker undercurrent, one that poses a significant threat to the sanctity of national sovereignty, particularly for a nation as steeped in individualistic and democratic ideals as the United States.

Globalism, at its core, is a doctrine of amalgamation. It advocates for a world where borders are less significant, and governance transcends national boundaries. While the intention might be cloaked in the noble pursuit of unity and shared prosperity, the reality often manifests as an erosion of the autonomy and unique character of nation-states, especially those with the historical gravitas of the United States.

The role of organizations like the World Economic Forum, NATO, and the United Nations (UN) in this globalist agenda cannot be understated. These entities, while ostensibly created to foster international cooperation and peace, have increasingly become platforms for a convergence of globalist ideals that often run counter to American values and interests.

The World Economic Forum, for instance, is frequently seen as a congregation of the global elite, dictating economic policies and practices that benefit a few at the expense of the many. This elitist approach, far removed from the everyday realities of the average American, raises questions about the priorities and motivations behind such globalist economic policies.

NATO, originally formed as a collective defense mechanism against common threats, has gradually expanded its scope and influence, sometimes acting in ways that complicate America's foreign policy objectives and constrain its strategic autonomy. The question then arises: to what extent should the United States be entangled in these alliances, which may require compromising its own interests for the sake of collective goals?

Similarly, the United Nations, an entity envisioned as a platform for international dialogue and conflict resolution, has often been criticized for its bureaucratic inefficiencies and a perceived bias against certain nations. The influence exerted by the UN in matters of international law and human rights has occasionally been at odds with the principles of American governance and the expectations of its populace.

In essence, the critique of globalism lies not in a rejection of international cooperation or a denial of the benefits of a connected world.

Rather, it is a call to acknowledge and address the disproportionate influence of these globalist entities on national sovereignty. It is about recognizing that in the pursuit of a borderless world, the unique voices of nations, especially one as distinct as the United States, risk being drowned out by a homogenizing global agenda.

It's abundantly clear that the balance between participating in the global community and preserving the fundamental aspects of national sovereignty is not just a matter of policy, but a pivotal question of identity and self-determination for the United States.

In the face of a world increasingly dominated by globalist agendas, the question that now confronts the United States is not just about the preservation of its sovereignty, but about the active steps needed to reclaim it. This isn't just a defensive maneuver; it's an assertive strategy to ensure that American interests, values, and autonomy stand robust against the tide of global integration that often seems to sweep national priorities aside.

First, the proposal to withdraw from globalist organizations is a bold yet necessary step. While this might seem like a retreat from the global stage, it is, in fact, a move toward reasserting control over our own policies and destiny. The United States must critically evaluate its involvement in organizations like the World Economic Forum, NATO, and the United Nations. Where do these alliances benefit the American people, and where do they hinder our ability to make independent decisions? It's about drawing lines that respect international cooperation but not at the expense of our sovereignty.

Second, enhancing our military capabilities and economic independence is pivotal. A strong military is not just about defense; it's about deterrence. It's about sending a clear message that American sovereignty is nonnegotiable. Economically, the United States needs to focus on self-reliance. This doesn't imply isolationism but rather the cultivation of a robust domestic economy that can compete on the global stage without being overly reliant on international systems that can be manipulated against American interests.

Border security is another cornerstone of sovereignty. A nation that cannot control its borders effectively relinquishes a part of its sovereignty. Strengthening border security isn't just about physical barriers; it's about smart technology, effective policy, and international cooperation that respects our borders.

The protection of American culture and values is paramount. In the race to embrace globalism, there's a risk of diluting the unique cultural identity that makes the United States what it is. While embracing diversity and change is a part of American DNA, it should not lead to the erosion of core values and traditions that have been the backbone of the nation.

This plan to reclaim American sovereignty is about striking a balance. It's about engaging with the world on terms that respect and prioritize American interests and values. It's a call for a strategic reevaluation of our international commitments, a reinforcement of our military and economic might, a firm stance on border security, and a commitment to preserving the cultural heritage that defines us.

It is a plan not just for the sake of policy but for the sake of the American spirit—a spirit that thrives on independence, self-determination, and the relentless pursuit of liberty and justice for all.

As we draw the curtain on this discourse about globalism and its encroachment on American sovereignty, it is imperative to crystallize the essence of what we have explored. This journey through the dense thicket of globalist agendas and their impact on our nation's autonomy is more than an academic exercise; it is a clarion call to awaken to the realities that confront us.

The threat posed by globalism to American sovereignty is not a specter looming on a distant horizon; it is a present and tangible challenge. It manifests in the subtle erosion of our ability to make independent decisions, in the gradual dilution of our national identity, and in the quiet surrender of the values that have long defined us.

This chapter is more than a critique; it is a rallying cry for action. The United States, with its storied history of independence and self-determination, cannot afford to be a passive player in the global arena, where its fate is decided by the whims and fancies of international conglomerates and foreign agendas.

We must reclaim control over our national destiny. This does not mean shunning international cooperation or rejecting the idea of a global community. Rather, it means engaging with the world on our own terms, in ways that preserve and protect our sovereignty. It means being vigilant about the agreements we enter, the alliances we forge, and the compromises we make.

The message is clear: our sovereignty is not for sale, our values are not up for negotiation, and our destiny is not to be dictated by external forces. The path forward is one of renewed commitment to the principles that have made the United States a beacon of freedom and democracy. It is a path of resilience, self-reliance, and a steadfast resolve to ensure that, in the concert of nations, the American voice is not just heard, but respected.

In the grand scheme of things, this chapter is but a footnote in the ongoing saga of our nation. Yet, it is a critical one. It serves as a reminder that the story of America is written not by external actors but by the indomitable spirit of its people, a spirit that refuses to be subdued by the siren songs of globalism. As we move forward, let us carry with us the unyielding determination to preserve that which makes us uniquely American—our sovereignty, our liberty, and our unwavering pursuit of a future where our nation remains the master of its destiny.

It is essential to anchor our understanding in the historical and philosophical contexts that have shaped nations. History, often a mirror reflecting the triumphs and tribulations of the past, offers us profound insights into the present discourse on national sovereignty.

The examination of nationalistic ideologies, particularly in the context of Adolf Hitler, is a delicate yet crucial part of this narrative. It's important to tread carefully here, recognizing the catastrophic consequences of extreme nationalism while also understanding the broader sociopolitical landscape that fostered such ideologies. Hitler's rise to power and the ensuing global conflict serve as a stark reminder of the dangers of unchecked nationalism and the importance of restraint in victory.

However, it is equally important to acknowledge that the nationalistic fervor of the early twentieth century was not an isolated phenomenon. It emerged from a complex interplay of economic hardship, political instability, and a profound sense of national humiliation and injustice. This historical context is crucial in understanding how nationalistic ideologies can take root and the impact they have on both domestic policies and global relations.

The relationship between state policy, economic conditions, and national identity is a recurring theme in history. From the Roman Empire to the modern era, the rise and fall of nations have often been closely tied to their economic prowess, political stability, and the strength of their national identity. The United States, with its unique blend of democracy and capitalism, has not been immune to these forces. The nation's history is replete with moments where the interplay of these elements has defined its course.

In this light, the current debate on globalism versus sovereignty is not just a question of political preference or ideology. It is rooted in a deeper philosophical discussion about the nature of statehood, the role of the individual in society, and the balance between national interests and global responsibilities.

The resurgence of nationalistic sentiments in various parts of the world today, including in the United States, is a reflection of this ongoing dialogue. It underscores the need to continually reassess and recalibrate our policies and alliances in a way that honors our history, respects our national identity, and acknowledges our role in the global community.

In the intricate dance between global and domestic policies, it's crucial to recognize how one moves the other in profound and often unexpected ways. The United States, a nation with a storied legacy on the world stage, finds itself at a crossroads where its domestic policies not only shape its global stature but are also, in turn, influenced by international dynamics.

The impact of global policies on domestic affairs is a tale as old as time, yet it's never been more relevant than in today's hyper-connected world. Take, for instance, trade agreements. These are not just contracts between nations; they are blueprints that can redefine entire industries, job markets, and economic landscapes within our borders. When we engage in agreements that prioritize global interests, often under the guise of progress and cooperation, we risk overlooking the American worker, the small businesses, and the local communities that form the backbone of our economy.

Conversely, our domestic policies send ripples across the globe. The political decisions we make, the cultural values we uphold, and the economic strategies we implement don't just stay within our borders; they echo in the halls of power worldwide. Our stance on issues like energy independence, for instance, doesn't just affect the price of gas at home; it influences global energy markets and foreign policy dynamics.

National unity and political will are the twin pillars upon which effective foreign policy rests. When the United States presents a united front, it wields considerable influence on the global stage. However, when internal divisions and political strife eclipse national interests, our global standing suffers. This isn't merely theoretical; history is replete with examples of how domestic upheaval has led to diminished influence abroad.

Thus, the interplay between our domestic policies and global standing is a delicate balancing act. It requires a nuanced understanding of both the international landscape and the home front. It necessitates leaders who can navigate this complex terrain with a vision that transcends political cycles and looks toward a future where American interests are protected and advanced both at home and abroad.

The relationship between global and domestic policies is symbiotic and dynamic. As we chart our course through these tumultuous waters, the need for policies that are thoughtful, farsighted, and firmly rooted in American interests has never been greater. It's about ensuring that the decisions we make within our borders strengthen our position beyond them, and that our actions on the global stage reflect and respect the values and aspirations of the American people.

Populist ideals, often misunderstood and sometimes maligned, are not about exclusion or aggression, but about a deep-seated sense of pride, identity, and commitment to the well-being of the nation.

At the heart of populist ideals lies the concept of a unified national identity and purpose. This is not about homogeneity or suppressing diversity; it is about fostering a sense of belonging, a shared commitment to the values and goals that define the American spirit. It's about an America where the interests and welfare of its citizens are the primary concerns of those in power.

The rejection of internationalism and certain democratic principles in favor of populist goals does not imply a disdain for global cooperation or democratic values. Rather, it underscores the necessity for policies and actions that first and foremost serve American interests. This is about prioritizing the needs of the American people over the demands of an often-nebulous international community.

The resurgence of populist sentiments across the globe, and particularly in the United States, is a response to the perceived excesses of globalism. It is a reaction to the erosion of sovereign rights, the dilution of cultural identities, and the loss of economic control to international entities that often do not have American interests at heart.

Advocating for populist ideals is not a step backward into isolationism; it's a stride toward ensuring that America does not lose its voice and its unique place in the world. It's about preserving the core values that have defined America since its inception—liberty, republicanism, individualism, and a relentless pursuit of happiness.

As we move forward, the importance of these populist ideals cannot be overstated. They are the compass that can guide the United States through the murky waters of global politics, ensuring that the nation remains strong, unified, and true to its founding principles. In a world where the lines between national interest and global agendas are increasingly blurred, a resurgence of national pride and a recommitment to nationalistic ideals are not just desirable, they are imperative.

Populist ideals should not be viewed through a lens of antagonism or fear, but as a beacon of hope and strength. They are the pillars upon which the future of American sovereignty and prosperity rests, ensuring that the nation continues to thrive in a rapidly changing world while remaining steadfast to the ideals that have long made America a beacon of freedom and opportunity on the global stage.

In an era where the forces of globalism continually test the bounds of national sovereignty, a strong, unified national ideology emerges not as an option, but as a necessity.

The importance of a robust and vibrant nationalistic perspective cannot be overstated. It is not about retreat into a shell of isolation or an arrogant dismissal of global cooperation. Rather, it's about reaffirming our commitment to the principles that have long defined the

American ethos—self-determination, liberty, and a relentless pursuit of the collective good of our people.

The need for domestic consolidation in the face of global pressures is more pressing than ever. This consolidation isn't merely political or economic; it's a consolidation of values, of a shared vision, and of a collective resolve to put America and its citizens at the forefront of every decision and policy. It is through this consolidation that the United States can project strength and confidence on the world stage, ensuring that its foreign policy objectives are not just heard but respected.

As we call for a resurgence of national pride and sovereignty, we invoke a vision of an America that is true to its founding ideals. It's a vision of a nation that embraces its unique identity, while also navigating the complexities of an interconnected world. This resurgence is not about diminishing others but about elevating the American spirit to new heights.

In essence, this populist perspective is not a relic of the past; it's a blueprint for the future. It's a guidepost for navigating the challenges of the twenty-first century, ensuring that America continues to shine as a beacon of hope, opportunity, and freedom. It's a clarion call to remember that while we may engage with the world, we must never lose sight of who we are and what we stand for.

Let us embrace it as a vital component of our national character, one that will enable us to forge a path that is both true to our heritage and responsive to the challenges of a dynamic global landscape. For in this bold embrace lies the key to a future where America not only endures but thrives, steadfast in its sovereignty and unwavering in its pursuit of a greater destiny.

## CHAPTER 16

# ONE AMERICAN CONVICTION

In the heart of America, amid the bustling cities and quiet rural land-scapes, there is a spirit that has long defined the nation. This spirit, born from the dreams of our forefathers and the struggles of generations, is the essence of the American identity. It is an identity steeped in values of freedom, determination, and a relentless pursuit of opportunity. Yet, in recent times, this proud legacy faces an unprecedented challenge—a growing wave of anti-American sentiment that threatens to erode the very foundations of our society.

It's time to confront this challenge head-on, to stand up and reclaim what it means to be American. Not in the sense of mere patriotism, but in the deeper understanding of our national ethos. This isn't about partisan politics or fleeting trends; it's about the core values that have been the bedrock of this great nation. Values like liberty, equality, and the unyielding belief in the potential of every individual.

But where do we begin? How do we counter the voices that demean our history and belittle our achievements? The answer lies not in aggression, but in affirmation—an affirmation of our culture, our heritage, and the enduring principles that have guided us through the toughest of times. It is here that we introduce a new path forward, a movement that transcends traditional political boundaries—the One American Party.

The American Populist Movement is more than just a political fad; it is a call to action. It represents a truly American effort to rekindle the American spirit that seems to be dimming in the hearts of many. This movement is not anchored in nostalgia, but in a clear-eyed recognition of what we can be as a nation. It's a vision that acknowledges our past, with all its triumphs and failings, while boldly striving for a future where every American can thrive.

Reclaiming our American identity is not about exclusion but about rediscovery. It's about rejecting the notion that to be critical of America's missteps is to be anti-American. Instead, it's about embracing the full spectrum of our history—the good and the bad—and using it as a foundation to build a more inclusive, stronger, and united country.

The road ahead is not without challenges. There will be voices that seek to divide us, ideologies that aim to distract us from our common goals. But the resilience of the American spirit has never faltered in the face of adversity. Now, more than ever, we need to channel that resilience into a renewed sense of purpose and identity.

Let this chapter be the first step in that journey. A journey to reclaim not just the America of the past, but to forge the America of tomorrow—an America that lives up to the ideals we hold dear. The formation of the One American Party is not the end, but a bold new beginning. It's a call to every American who believes in the promise of this great nation to stand up, to be heard, and to take part in shaping our collective destiny. Together, we can turn the tide and reawaken the true spirit of America.

At the core of the American journey lies a powerful truth, one that resonates through the corridors of history and in the hearts of those who dare to dream—the truth of self-claiming. It is in this very act of self-assertion where the American spirit finds its most potent expression. This is not about empty boasting or shallow pride; it's about a deep, unwavering belief in the values and ideals that have shaped this nation.

To claim oneself as American is to embrace a heritage that is as diverse as it is profound. This land, forged by the hands of countless cultures, ethnicities, and beliefs, is a testament to the strength that comes from assimilation. Our cultural heritage is not a monolith, but a mosaic, rich with varied histories and experiences. Each piece, each story, adds to the grandeur of the American tapestry. Yet, in today's climate, there seems to be an insidious trend to belittle this heritage, to paint America with a brush of negativity and shame.

This is not just inaccurate; it's an injustice to the generations that have built, defended, and enriched this nation. Rejecting these negative perceptions is more than an act of defiance; it's an act of honor—an honor to those who believed in the American Dream and toiled to make it a reality. We owe it to them and to ourselves to uphold the true image of America, an image that reflects resilience, innovation, and an enduring pursuit of freedom.

Upholding American rights and values is fundamental in this process of self-claiming. These rights and values are not abstract concepts to be relegated to history books; they are the living, breathing essence of our daily lives. They are what allow us to speak our minds, to worship freely, to strive for excellence, and to stand up for what we believe is right. In a world that often seems to be shifting under the weight of moral relativism, these values stand as a beacon of clarity and conviction.

But let's be clear: claiming oneself as American is not a passive act. It demands engagement, awareness, and a willingness to confront challenges head-on. It involves educating ourselves about our history, engaging in constructive dialogue, and participating actively in the shaping of our future. It's about taking pride not just in our achievements, but also in our ability to overcome our failures and learn from them.

This chapter of reclaiming our American identity is not just about looking back with reverence; it's about looking forward with purpose. It's about reasserting our place in the world, not out of a sense of superiority, but from a desire to contribute, to lead, and to inspire. As we stand at this crossroads, the path we choose must be guided by the enduring principles that have served as the bedrock of this great nation.

So let us claim ourselves as Americans with pride and conviction. Let us embrace our heritage, uphold our values, and step boldly into the future. This is not a journey of isolation but of reaffirmation—a reaffirmation that we are, indeed, a people defined by our resilience, and our unwavering commitment to the ideals of liberty and justice for all. In this act of claiming, we rediscover the essence of what it truly means to be American.

A disturbing narrative has taken hold in American politics, one that unfairly characterizes America as a land steeped in oppression and injustice. This portrayal, often echoed in academic circles and media outlets, seeks to paint the American story with broad strokes of condemnation and reproach. It's a narrative that not only distorts our history but also undermines our national identity.

However, the truth, often overlooked, is far more complex and inspiring. America, in its essence, is not a tale of unending oppression, but a saga of continual struggle and triumph over adversity. This nation was founded on principles of liberty and justice, and while we have faltered at times, our history is replete with examples of moral courage and progress.

Rejecting anti-Americanism isn't about ignoring our past mistakes; it's about acknowledging them while also celebrating our collective efforts to overcome them. It's about recognizing that America, at its heart, has always been a work in progress—a nation perpetually striving to live up to its founding ideals. The narrative of America as inherently oppressive ignores the countless men and women who have fought tirelessly to expand the scope of freedom and equality. From the abolitionists to populists, our history is marked by individuals and movements that have pushed America closer to its ideals.

Standing up for American values and the American way of life means acknowledging this enduring spirit of progress and reform. It means understanding that American culture, far from being monolithic, is a vibrant tapestry woven from the threads of many traditions, beliefs, and histories. This cultural richness is something to be celebrated, not denigrated.

To effectively counter the narrative of anti-Americanism, we must engage in a culture of affirmation—affirming the values of freedom and equal opportunity that define the American experience. This involves a proactive approach to education, where American history is taught not as a series of condemnations but as a dynamic story of growth and improvement. It also calls for a reevaluation of how the media and entertainment industries portray American life and values. We must strive for a balanced representation that reflects the complexity and diversity of the American experience.

The cultural rejection of anti-Americanism is, at its core, a call to embrace a more nuanced and accurate understanding of our nation's story. It's an invitation to celebrate the strides we've made while acknowledging the work that still lies ahead. By doing so, we honor not just our past but also our potential as a nation committed to liberty, justice, and the pursuit of a more perfect union. In this rejection lies the affirmation of an America that is ever-evolving, resilient, and true to its foundational principles.

A narrative as old as the nation itself is playing out with unrelenting predictability—the dominance of two major political parties, the Democrats and the Republicans. These parties, which have long claimed to represent the entirety of the American political spectrum, have become entrenched symbols of an establishment out of touch with the people it purports to serve. It's time to confront this reality with clear eyes and acknowledge that these traditional power structures are no longer adequate to address the complexities and challenges of modern America.

The critique of these establishment parties is not rooted in partisanship but in a sober assessment of their performance. Time and again, we've witnessed these parties succumb to internal politicking, special interest groups, and a detachment from the everyday concerns of the average American. They have become mired in a cycle of reactive politics, more focused on countering each other than on addressing the real issues facing the nation.

The Democratic Party, with its shifting ideologies and policies, often appears disconnected from the foundational principles that once defined it. Meanwhile, the Republican Party, grappling with its identity in a rapidly changing world, frequently seems caught between the values it professes and the realities it faces. This dichotomy within and between the parties has led to a stagnation in American political discourse, where the true needs and aspirations of the American people are often overshadowed by partisan battles and rhetorical grandstanding.

The American Populist Movement is born out of a recognition that the existing political paradigm is inadequate for the challenges we face today. This new One American Party of sorts is not just another addition to the political fray; it is a fundamental rethinking of how politics should be conducted in America. It seeks to transcend the binary constraints of the current system, advocating for policies and ideals that resonate with a broad spectrum of Americans.

The vision for the One American Party is simple yet revolutionary: to place the interests and well-being of the American people above all else. This means a commitment to policies that foster economic growth, social stability, and a renewed focus on the principles of liberty and justice for all.

In rejecting the establishment parties, the One American Party represents a return to the fundamental values that have always been at the core of the American experiment. It is a call to move beyond the divisiveness and gridlock that have come to characterize our politics and to embrace a more unified, pragmatic approach to governance.

This rejection is not an end but a beginning—the start of a new chapter in American political life. It is an invitation to all Americans, regardless of their political affiliations, to join in creating a political movement that truly represents the will and aspirations of the American people. The formation of the One American Party is a bold step toward realizing the full potential of America, a step toward a government that is of the people, by the people, and for the people.

In the annals of American history, civil disobedience has stood as a bastion of the people's power. It is the tool of the citizen, the expression of the individual against the might of the establishment when it veers off the path of justice and righteousness. Today, in the face of laws and mandates that many feel trample upon their fundamental rights, civil disobedience emerges not just as a choice, but as a duty for those committed to the preservation of liberty and individual freedom.

The concept of civil disobedience harks back to the founding of the nation, where defiance against unjust laws was not just seen as acceptable, but necessary. The Boston Tea Party, a hallmark of American revolutionary spirit, was an act of civil disobedience. It set the stage for a nation that would not shy away from standing up to authority when that authority becomes oppressive or overreaching.

But let's be unequivocally clear—advocating for civil disobedience is not an endorsement of chaos or lawlessness. True civil disobedience is a calculated, conscientious decision to resist unjust laws through peaceful, nonviolent means. It is a form of protest deeply rooted in a commitment to justice and a belief in the power of the individual to enact change.

In contemporary America, the call for civil disobedience is a response to a growing sense of disenfranchisement and frustration with an establishment seen as increasingly autocratic. Whether it's mandates that infringe on personal freedoms or laws that are perceived to violate constitutional rights, there is a growing segment of the population that feels compelled to take a stand.

It's essential, however, to distinguish between legitimate civil disobedience and mere anarchy. The former is a principled stand, often taken at great personal cost, in the name of a greater good. It is driven by a respect for the rule of law, even as it challenges specific laws. The latter, on the other hand, is the abandonment of all societal rules and often leads to destruction and chaos.

The effectiveness of civil disobedience is not measured in immediate results but in its ability to spark dialogue and bring about change over time. From the Civil Rights Movement to recent protests for various causes, history has shown that peaceful resistance can lead to significant societal shifts. It is a reminder to those in power that the will of the people is not to be taken lightly and that the true strength of a republic lies in its ability to accommodate dissenting voices.

As we consider the role of civil disobedience in today's society, it's imperative to approach it with a sense of responsibility and a clear understanding of its implications. It is a powerful tool, one that should be wielded with care and respect for the principles that underpin our society. In advocating for the rights and liberties we hold dear, we must always strive to uphold the very values that define us as a nation committed to liberty, justice, and the rule of law.

Nothing is more fundamental to America as a nation or to American culture as the fierce protection of the right to free speech. It is the cornerstone of our republic, the guardian of our liberties, and the facilitator of our progress. In today's climate, where the very notion of free speech is under siege, it's more crucial than ever to understand and uphold this essential right.

Free speech is not merely a constitutional guarantee; it is the lifeblood of a free society. It empowers the individual, enables the exchange of ideas, and fosters the kind of robust debate that is critical for a healthy democracy. When voices are silenced, when opinions are suppressed, we don't just lose words or ideas; we lose the very essence of what makes our society vibrant and dynamic.

But let's face the uncomfortable truth: the right to free speech is increasingly being challenged. There are growing calls for censorship, for the policing of ideas and the quelling of dissenting views under the guise of maintaining social harmony or protecting sensibilities. This is a dangerous path, one that leads to the erosion of our freedoms and the homogenization of our thoughts.

The importance of free speech must be viewed through the lens of its role in fostering societal growth. It is through the clash of differing ideas, the contention of opposing viewpoints, that we find the seeds of progress. Great movements in history, from civil rights to women's suffrage, were propelled by the ability to speak out against the status quo, to challenge prevailing norms and advocate for change.

The context of speech in our society has evolved dramatically with the advent of digital platforms and social media. These new mediums have revolutionized the way we communicate, offering unprecedented opportunities for expression. Yet, they also pose unique challenges to free speech, including issues around privacy, misinformation, and the control of information by a few dominant players.

In addressing these challenges, it's imperative to never compromise the protection of free speech.

The preservation of free speech is not just the responsibility of governments or institutions; it's a duty that falls on each of us as individuals. We must be vigilant in defending our right to speak, and equally important, our obligation to listen. We must be willing to engage with ideas that challenge us, to consider viewpoints that differ from our own, and to do so with a spirit of respect and understanding.

As we navigate the complexities of the modern world, the importance of free speech remains undiminished. It is the foundation upon which we build our knowledge, shape our beliefs, and define our identities. In upholding this fundamental right, we uphold the very principles that make us free—the principles of liberty, of individuality, and of the relentless pursuit of truth. Let us not forget that in a nation where voices are free to speak, the spirit of liberty thrives.

America's story, often lionized yet sometimes vilified, is a tapestry woven from threads of ambition, struggle, triumph, and yes, at times, tragedy. To fully comprehend the challenges we face today—from the erosion of individual liberties to the debate over America's role in a globalized world—we must look back at the historical currents that have shaped our nation.

The impact of globalism on America cannot be overstated. This phenomenon, which has accelerated in recent decades, has fundamentally altered the landscape of our economy, our society, and our politics. The American experience, once defined by a clear sense of identity and purpose, now grapples with the complexities of a world where borders are less defined, and identities are increasingly fluid.

This brings us to the American question of living space and rights. The notion of "living space," historically rooted in the pursuit of the American Dream, has evolved. It's no longer just about physical space or geographical expansion but about navigating the space within a global context. How does America assert its identity and protect its interests in a world where economic, cultural, and political landscapes are constantly shifting?

This question is not just rhetorical; it's deeply rooted in the historical journey of America. From the early days of the republic, where the frontier symbolized endless possibility, to the post–World War era, where America emerged as a global superpower, each phase of our history has brought with it new challenges and opportunities. Today, as we stand in the midst of the digital revolution and an era of unprecedented global connectivity, the question morphs yet again.

The debate over globalism and its implications is not just an academic one. It affects real policies and, more importantly, real people. Jobs, industries, and entire communities have felt the impact of a global economy. The decisions we make, the policies we implement, and the leaders we choose will determine how well America navigates this global landscape. Will we retreat into isolationism, or will we embrace the global stage while still maintaining our unique identity and values?

Understanding our history is crucial in making these decisions. We must learn from the past—from the successes and the failures—to chart a course for the future. America has always been at its best when it's adaptable, innovative, and true to its foundational principles. The challenge, then, is not just to react to the forces of globalism but to shape them in a way that is consistent with our values and beneficial to our people.

In this historical context lies the road map for our future. It's a map that calls for a reassertion of American values, a reevaluation of our role in the world, and a renewed commitment to the principles that have made us a beacon of hope and opportunity. As we move forward, let us do so with an eye on the past, a clear vision for the present, and an unwavering hope for the future.

As the lines between domestic issues and foreign policy increasingly blur, America stands at a crucial juncture. The decisions we make, the stances we adopt, both internally and on the global stage, will indelibly shape the future of this nation. It's a moment that demands not just clarity of vision but a steadfast adherence to our core principles.

Internally, America faces a myriad of challenges. Economic struggles, evidenced by the plight of the working class, the erosion of the middle class, and the stark disparities in wealth, are more than just financial issues; they are a reflection of our societal values. Political division, a scourge that seems to deepen with each passing day, is not just a disagreement of ideas but a fundamental schism in our understanding of what America is and should be. These internal challenges are a clarion call for introspection and action.

We must ask ourselves: What kind of America do we want to live in? Do we want a nation where the divide between the haves and the have-nots widens relentlessly? Where the political discourse is so polarized that common ground seems like a distant memory? The answers to these questions are crucial because they will guide our policies, shape our society, and define our identity as a nation.

Turning to the external aspect, America's relationship with the rest of the world is equally complex. In an era where global dynamics are constantly shifting, our foreign policy must be both principled and pragmatic. The rise of new powers, the changing nature of global threats, and the challenges of international cooperation require a nuanced approach. America must navigate these waters with a clear understanding of its interests and a firm commitment to its values.

Our stance on globalism and globalist organizations is particularly contentious. While global cooperation is essential in addressing issues like international trade, it should not come at the cost of our sovereignty or our values. America's engagement with global institutions must be based on the interests of the American people.

The proposals for peace and security, both at home and abroad, must reflect a deep understanding of these complexities. We need strategies that are forward-thinking, that protect our interests, and that promote stability and prosperity both for our citizens and for the world at large. This requires a departure from simplistic, one-size-fits-all solutions and a move toward policies that are tailored to the nuanced realities of the twenty-first century.

As we chart our course, both internally and externally, we must do so with an unwavering commitment to the principles that have defined America since its inception—liberty, republicanism, and the pursuit of happiness. These principles should not just guide our domestic policies but also our interactions on the global stage. In a world rife with complexity and uncertainty, they serve as our North Star, guiding us toward a future that is prosperous, secure, and true to the American spirit.

In these times of unprecedented division and discord, the call for American unity and support resonates with a sense of urgency that cannot be ignored. This is not a mere appeal to sentimental patriotism, but a pragmatic recognition of the fact that a house divided against itself cannot stand. The strength of America has always been found in its unity, in the ability of its people to come together in pursuit of common goals, despite their differences.

Reflecting on the leadership and achievements of our past, we see a legacy of unity in the face of adversity. From the early settlers forging a new nation, to the generations that faced down the specters of fascism and communism, America has always been at its greatest when its people were united. These achievements were not the result of a single individual or party, but the collective effort of a people united by a shared belief in the promise of America.

Today, however, the fabric of American unity is fraying. Political polarization, cultural divides, and social media echo chambers have created a landscape where common ground seems increasingly scarce. In this environment, the call for unity is not just about bridging political divides; it's about rediscovering the shared values that define us as Americans. Values like freedom, justice, and the pursuit of happiness.

The request for American support extends beyond mere rhetoric. It's a call to action for every citizen, regardless of their political affiliations, to actively participate in the process of governance and community building. This involves engaging in constructive dialogue, being informed about the issues, and voting in elections. It's about being involved in local communities, supporting initiatives that promote unity and understanding, and standing against forces that seek to divide us.

As we look to the future, we do so with a recognition of the challenges that lie ahead. The world is changing rapidly, and America must adapt to remain a leader on the global stage. This adaptation requires the support of its people—support not just for specific policies or leaders, but for the enduring ideals that make America unique.

In calling for unity and support, we are not asking for uniformity of thought or blind allegiance. We are asking for a renewed commitment to the principles of freedom. It's about putting aside our minor differences and focusing on the larger picture—the picture of an America that is prosperous, secure, and a beacon of hope for the world.

This call for unity and support is, at its heart, a call to rekindle the American spirit. It's a call to remember that, despite our diverse backgrounds and beliefs, we are all bound by a common destiny. It's a reminder that, together, there is no challenge too great, no obstacle too daunting. Let us answer this call with the courage, determination, and optimism that have always been the hallmarks of the American character. Let us come together, not just as a collection of individuals, but as a united people, committed to building a brighter future for ourselves and for generations to come.

The call for Americans to reclaim their identity is not a journey backward to a bygone era, but a stride forward into a future that is yet to be written. A future where every American, regardless of their background or beliefs, can find common cause in the pursuit of a better nation and a better world.

The rise of American populism, then, is not just a political movement; it transcends politics. It's an expression of the American spirit, a spirit that refuses to be cowed by challenges, that rises above divisiveness, and that seeks to unite rather than divide. This movement is an embodiment of the belief that, despite our differences, we share a common destiny, a destiny that can only be fulfilled when we work together in harmony and unwavering conviction.

Let us not be daunted by the challenges that lie ahead. Instead, let us be inspired by the possibilities that await us. The road to a more perfect union is never easy; it is fraught with obstacles and setbacks. But the history of America is a testament to the triumph of the human spirit over adversity. It's a story of a people who, time and again, have risen to meet the challenges of their day with courage, determination, and an unwavering commitment to Americanism.

Let this not be an end, but a beginning. A beginning of a renewed commitment to the values that define us, a rekindled spirit of unity and purpose, and a resolute determination to forge an America that lives up to the highest ideals of its founding. Together, as one nation, under God, indivisible, let us march forward into the future, confident in our ability to overcome any obstacle, united in our pursuit of a brighter tomorrow. This is our charge, this is our mission, and together, we shall prevail.

# EPILOGUE:
# A POPULIST PRESIDENT

This book represents the silenced majority and has dissected the ideological battles and cultural wars that have torn at the fabric of American society. We have witnessed a concerted effort to dilute our cherished values and surrender our hard-won freedoms to the altar of globalism and leftist orthodoxy.

In this dire hour, when the very essence of our national identity is under siege, America calls for a champion: a defender of liberty and prosperity. That champion, as we have seen through action and results, through trials and triumphs, is none other than Donald J. Trump. His presidency was marked by an unapologetic affirmation of American greatness, a relentless pursuit of prosperity for all citizens, and a formidable stance against the forces seeking to undermine our sovereignty.

As the 2024 presidential election approaches, it is imperative that we, the true custodians of American heritage, rally once more under the banner that Trump has boldly carried. The choice before us is stark, and the stakes could not be higher. It is not merely a political contest but a pivotal battle for the soul of our nation, a struggle to reclaim and restore the foundational principles that have made this country a beacon of hope and freedom across the globe.

Donald Trump's re-election in 2024 is not merely desirable; it is essential. It is the linchpin upon which the future of our republic hinges.

Trump's leadership is our bulwark against the encroaching shadows of tyranny and decline. Together, we must seize this moment to ensure that America remains forever free, forever proud, and forever resolute.

Leadership—not merely the holding of an office, but the bold, decisive action that defines true statesmanship—is the cornerstone upon which the fate of nations pivots. President Trump exemplified this type of leadership during his presidency, steering America with a firm hand and clear vision, distinguishing himself as a paragon of resolve and determination.

Throughout his initial term, President Trump's leadership was characterized by an unyielding commitment to America's economic vitality, national security, and cultural heritage. He engineered a historic economic resurgence, with record-low unemployment rates across all demographics, a booming stock market, and a revitalization of industries long left to languish in neglect. His policies were not shaped by the winds of political expediency but by the bedrock principles of free enterprise and fair trade.

On the international stage, Trump's leadership reasserted American sovereignty. He challenged adversaries and renegotiated trade deals that had siphoned off American wealth and jobs for decades. His stance was clear: America would no longer be taken advantage of, but instead demand respect and fair dealings from both friends and foes alike. This approach not only bolstered our economic standing but also restored our nation's dignity on the global platform.

Contrast this with the current administration's period of leadership, marked by indecision, retreat, and capitulation. Under their watch, we have witnessed a resurgence of threats both old and new, foreign and domestic, from the emboldening of rogue states to the unchecked rise of globalist agendas that seek to erode national borders and sovereignty. Domestically, policies have shifted toward the appeasement of interest groups and the proliferation of regulatory overreach, all the while stifling innovation and sapping the entrepreneurial spirit.

The stark difference in outcomes between these two approaches underscores a fundamental truth: that leadership matters. It is not merely about making decisions but making the *right* decisions—the hard decisions that require both courage and foresight. The type of leadership that Trump provided—and must again wield—is rooted in a profound understanding of America's foundational values and an unwavering commitment to its future prosperity.

America stands at a crossroads, facing challenges that will define the course of our future. To navigate these challenges, we need a leader who has demonstrated the capacity to handle the rigors of the presidency and the resolve to act decisively. We need a leader who can restore the momentum of national renewal that began under Trump's first term.

In re-electing President Trump, this is not just a political choice but a statement of our commitment to the principles upon which our country was built: liberty, prosperity, and strength.

Trump's tenure in the Oval Office was distinguished not merely by his policies but by his unrelenting defense of the principles that define America: freedom, individualism, and patriotism. These are not mere abstract ideals but the lifeblood of our republic, the guiding stars that have steered our nation through the annals of history.

Culturally, Trump stood against the forces of cancel culture and the radical left's attempt to rewrite our history. He understood that a nation that loses grip on its past forfeits its future. His actions in establishing the 1776 Commission were a direct response to the destructive narratives that sought to sow division and self-loathing among our people. This initiative aimed to promote a patriotic education, fostering a renewed appreciation for Americanism.

The current administration's approach has often seemed at odds with these core principles. Their policies have frequently favored international consensus over American interests, undermining our sovereignty and compromising our security. They have shown a troubling propensity to engage with cultural narratives that divide rather than unite, promoting a version of America's story that diminishes its achievements and magnifies its failures without context or balance.

As the 2024 election approaches, the need for a leader who is unafraid to stand up for America, who can articulate and defend its values with clarity and conviction, is critical. President Trump has proven that he is that leader. His record speaks of a president who does not merely occupy an office but embodies the spirit of the American ethos. He has demonstrated the courage to lead from the front, to stand firm against the onslaught of criticism, and to uphold the tenets of freedom and justice that have made America a beacon of hope for the world.

Under Trump's leadership, America witnessed a renaissance in its economic fortunes. Tax reforms were implemented with precision to unshackle the productive forces of the economy. By significantly lowering tax rates for individuals and corporations, Trump's policies incentivized investment, expanded businesses, and increased take-home pay for millions of American workers. These measures not only bolstered consumer confidence but also stimulated a surge in job creation, reducing unemployment to historic lows across all demographics, including among African Americans, Hispanics, and women.

The stock market responded with record-breaking profits, reflecting investor confidence in an economy unimpeded by excessive regulatory constraints. Trump's aggressive stance on deregulation untangled businesses from the red tape that previously stifled innovation and growth. This approach rejuvenated industries, particularly manufacturing and energy—sectors that had been in decline, and thus breathing new life into the American industrial spirit.

In contrast, the economic strategies of the current administration have seen a retreat from such gains. Their policies have often favored regulatory proliferation and international appeasement, which have contributed to economic stagnation and uncertainty. Supply chain disruptions, rising inflation, and diminishing global competitiveness have become the hallmarks of their tenure, eroding the economic foundation rebuilt under Trump.

President Trump's policies reinforced the thin blue line that guards our communities, ensuring that law enforcement officials were respected, supported, and adequately funded. He vehemently opposed the dangerous calls to defund our police forces, recognizing that such measures would only lead to increased crime and chaos, as has been demonstrated in cities where such policies have been enacted.

Trump's administration also took significant strides in combating the scourge of illegal drugs and human trafficking networks that have threatened the social fabric of our nation. Initiatives to secure our southern border were not merely about immigration; they were about stemming the tide of criminal enterprises that exploit open borders to the detriment of American citizens and the migrants exploited by these ruthless cartels.

Moreover, Trump's leadership saw the enactment of several key criminal justice reforms, such as the First Step Act, which sought to balance the scales of justice, proving that law and order can coexist with fairness and compassion. These reforms aimed to reduce recidivism and ensure a fair chance at redemption for those who seek to reintegrate into society, reflecting a holistic approach to public safety.

Contrasting sharply with the current administration, the decline in public safety is evident. Their reluctance to confront the reality of crime, their hesitation to fully back law enforcement, and their indulgence of progressive policies that prioritize ideology over safety have left our cities vulnerable and our citizens at risk. The results have been stark: rising crime rates, demoralized police forces, communities living in fear.

The 2024 election is a referendum on the very essence of what it means to be American. It is about choosing a path that reaffirms our steadfast commitment to the principles that have defined us: liberty, prosperity, and indefatigable strength. President Trump has not only articulated a vision resonant with these enduring values but has demonstrated the fortitude to implement it amidst the tumult and opposition that characterizes our current political climate.

This call to action is for every American who believes in the promise of our great nation. It is for those who recognize the necessity of experienced, decisive leadership in a world that grows increasingly complex and dangerous. It is for those who value the sanctity of law and order, the importance of a thriving economy, and the preservation of freedoms that have long been the cornerstone of our national identity. It is a call to those who have witnessed the erosion of these pillars under current governance and yearn for their restoration.

In Trump, we see a leader unafraid to wield the mantle of American exceptionalism, a commander in chief who stands undeterred against global pressures and ideological distortions. His policies are not merely plans on paper; they are commitments carved in the spirit of American determination, designed to propel our nation forward on a trajectory of prosperity and influence.

We stand at a crossroads, where our choices will either anchor us in the mires of mediocrity and division or propel us toward a future replete with unparalleled greatness. Let us choose the path of strength and unity. Let us choose a leader proven to navigate the tumultuous waters of global complexities with unmatched prowess. Let us re-elect President Trump and reclaim the promise of America not only for ourselves but for the generations that will inherit this great nation. Let us move forward with the courage of our convictions, united in our cause and inspired by the promise of a brighter American future.

In the spirit of indomitable resolve that defines us as a people, let us march to the polls in 2024, casting our votes for Trump and, in essence, for America. Together, emboldened by our shared values and hopes, we will write the next chapter of our American story—one of renewed strength, honor, and global leadership. Let us make this decision with the clear vision and firm resolve that the times demand, ensuring that America remains forever the land of the free and the home of the brave.

big business and big government, the military-intelligence-industrial complex—which is hell-bent on eternal war—and the all-out assault on free speech and the Second Amendment.

The good news is that these plans are destined to fail, if we wake up to the anti-human future the globalists have planned for us. The globalists hate freedom, and what they hate the most is the greatest freedom document in human history, the United States Constitution. Jones does not shy away from the darker parts of American history—the way we have been systematically deceived by the intelligence agencies since their assassination of President John F. Kennedy—but he provides example after example of people who have broken free from the matrix of lies to tell the truth.

The people the globalists fear the most are the members of their own systems of control, who wake up and then decide to act against the machine. The globalists believe they've planned for every possible contingency, but they hadn't counted on the conscience and love of truth, which lives in the souls of good people.

St. Augustine once wrote: "The truth is like a lion; you don't have to defend it. Let it loose; it will defend itself." No figure in our modern times has roared louder against the enemies of freedom than Alex Jones. In the calm and dispassionate style that made his first book, *The Great Reset: And the War for the World*, such a smash hit, Alex lays out the flaws in the plans of the globalists and how they seek to create a world in direct opposition to God's plans for our glorious human future. But God consistently works His will in our world, even through imperfect individuals like Donald Trump, Alex Jones, or you.

If you want to read one book this year to understand your world and help lead humanity to the next great human renaissance, you need to order this book today.

$32.50 Hardcover Jacket · ISBN 978-1-5107-7902-0

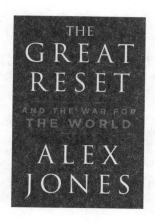

**The Great Reset**
**And the War for the World**
by Alex Jones

*If you really want to know what's happening in the world, this is the one book you must read now. Alex Jones is the most censored man on the planet and you should ask yourself why that is. There is a powerful authoritarian takeover in process that is seeking to capture the entire human system and turn it into an artificial factory farm controlled system. We are in a war for the future of the world. In this book, you will hear from the world's elites, from their own mouths, what they are planning for you and your families and you will learn what you can do to fight it.*

From central bankers, corporate billionaires, and corrupted government officials, global elites have been organizing a historic war on humanity under a trans-humanist, scientific dictatorship. Alex Jones was the first major figure to expose the World Economic Forum's agenda. He has dedicated the last 30 years of his life to studying The Great Reset, conducting tens of thousands of interviews with top-level scientists, politicians, and military officials in order to reverse engineer their secrets and help awaken humanity.

*The Great Reset: And the War for the World* chronicles the history of the global elites' rise to power and reveals how they've captured the governments of the world and financed The Great Reset to pave the way for The New World Order.

Once dubbed a conspiracy theory, but now openly promoted by the most powerful corporations and governments, The Great Reset is a planned attempt to redistribute all the world's wealth and power into the hands of banks, corporations, billionaires, and The World Economic Forum.

If you read one book in a lifetime, this is it. In *The Great Reset: And the War for the World*, you will discover from the self-appointed controllers of the planet in their own words, their plan for what they call the final revolution, or The Great Reset.

The only way this corporate fascist conspiracy can succeed is if the people of the world are not aware of it. And this book lays out their sinister blueprint and how to stop it. While many great books have been written to help awaken people to this sinister agenda, no author has ever spent as much time and research on The Great Reset as Alex Jones.

T*he Great Reset: And the War for the World* is the undisputed trailblazer for understanding what's happening and how to stop it.

$32.50 Hardcover Jacket · ISBN 978-1-5107-7404-9

# COMING SOON FROM WAR ROOM BOOKS!

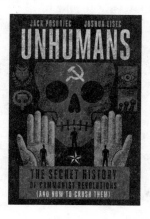

**Unhumans**
**The Secret History of Communist Revolutions (and How to Crush Them)**
Jack Posobiec and Joshua Lisec

If you don't understand communist revolutions, you aren't ready for what's coming.

The old rules are over. The old order is over. Accusations are evidence. Activism means bigotry and hate. Criminals are allowed to roam free. Citizens are locked up. An appetite for vengeance is unleashed—to deplatform, debank, destroy. This is the daily news, yet none of it's new. Patterns from the past make sense of our present. They also foretell a terrifying future we might be condemned to endure.

For nearly 250 years, far-left uprisings have followed the same battle plans—from the first call for change to last innocent executed, from denial a revolution is even happening to declaration of the new order. *Unhumans* takes readers on a shocking, sweeping, and succinct journey through history to share the untold stories of radical takeovers that textbooks don't teach.

And there is one conclusion: We're in a new revolution right now.

But this is not a book about ideology or politics. *Unhumans* reveals that communism, socialism, Marxism, and all other radical-isms are not philosophies but tactics—tactics that are specifically designed to unleash terror on everyday people and revoke their human rights to life, liberty, and property. These are the forces of unhumanity. This is what they do. Every. Single. Time. *Unhumans* steals their playbook, breaks apart their strategies piece by piece, and lays out the tactics of what it takes to fight back—and win, using real-world examples.

*Unhumans* is the essential read for every concerned citizen both of the US and worldwide. We must stop what is coming.

$29.99 Hardcover Jacket · ISBN 978-1-64821-085-3